The Modern Guide to College

The Modern Guide to College

Essential Advice for the Most Important Years of Your Life

Dr. Kent Ingle

Fedd Books
P.O. Box 341973
Austin, TX 78734
www.thefeddagency.com

Published in association with The Fedd Agency, Inc., a literary agency.

ISBN: 978-1-949784-22-0
eISBN: 978-1-949784-23-7

Printed in the United States of America

First Edition 15 14 13 12 11 / 10 9 8 7 6 5 4 3 2

Contents

Section 2 – During College

Activities
Looking Out for **You**

Introduction

AS THE PRESIDENT OF SOUTHEASTERN University for the last eight years, I have presided over thousands of students and watched one of the country's best Christian universities flourish. Now, you might think at age eighteen I enrolled at a top-ten college, rubbed shoulders with established families, and somehow got my name on a short-list for university president as a part of my detailed ten-year plan. You wouldn't think that at age eighteen I attended a local community college while working as the lead sports broadcaster at the NBC affiliate TV station in Bakersfield, California. You especially wouldn't think that I hadn't the slightest idea of what I wanted to do with my life as a high school senior, but that's the truth—as a young man in high school I was thinking about college, but really didn't know what I should study or what I wanted to do with my life. You may be asking yourself now, *and he's president of a university? How in the world did that happen?* I'm a living testament that life is a journey that often doesn't end up how you expected.

When I graduated from high school, I knew I had a passion for communication and loved helping people. I did not have a specific plan or even idea, however, on how to combine these two things in my life and form a future career from my passions. In the meantime, I determined that I could at least get started in the right direction by taking some general courses at my local community college. This place wasn't glamorous—not like heading off to some Ivy League university—but it was very productive and a whole lot less expensive.

To develop my passions, I took basic English and Speech courses. After my first speech, the instructor invited me to her office and told me that I had done a fine job and, in her opinion, thought I had a gift for public speaking. She wanted me to think about pursuing a career in a communications field. Best of all, she told me about an internship at the local NBC affiliate TV station in Bakersfield. I secured an internship and began working directly with the lead sports broadcaster—learning everything I could. From my internship, I discovered I quite enjoyed broadcast journalism and decided to take a course on Broadcast Writing, which turned out to be a good choice—my instructor in that class was the news director for the same TV station where I was an intern (major brownie points).

About three months into the internship, the TV station's sports broadcaster left for another job. I had developed relationships with the people at the news station and took a big risk asking the news director if he would consider me for that job. He let me do a practice story on camera and offered me a job on the spot. I could hardly believe it—I was only eighteen! This was the beginning of my first career as a sports broadcaster, and the skills I learned helped shape my future as the president of Southeastern University.

In the years that followed, I had the unusual experience of my career actually dictating where I continued my education. Eventually, I ended up as a sports broadcaster at a network station in Los Angeles and finally—much to my parents' relief—finished my bachelor's degree at a nearby university.

After a number of years in broadcasting, I felt a call to enter local church ministry. I realized that more education would be beneficial, particularly if I wanted to become a lead pastor. Since I had been in church work for a time, I had developed a fairly specific idea of the subject matter I wanted from a graduate degree—a study program that would really help me accomplish my goals in a church setting. So, I went looking for a graduate program that would provide me with a blend of church history, biblical studies, and leadership. It took some effort, but eventually I found exactly what I desired. As I continued in my ministerial career, I wanted to improve my leadership abilities so I could lead the organizations that I was responsible for effectively. So, I enrolled and eventually earned my doctorate in ministry, with a focus on organizational leadership. Again, at each stage of my life, my education wasn't about trying to unlock some future door, but about bringing *my best self* to the context. And what happened when I made that my primary focus? All of a sudden, doors that I never thought I could enter started to open.

One day, when I was working as a pastor, I was approached to become the dean of a college at a private liberal arts university. Me! A guy who went to community college and never taught a college class in my life—a dean! So, I did that for a number of years, using everything I had learned in both broadcasting and pastoring to expand and grow the college. Then one day, out of the blue, I received a call from the Presidential Search Committee of Southeastern University—and I guess you can say the rest is history!

It might be surprising, but you probably have

a lot in common with a president of a university. At your age, I wasn't sure of myself and certainly had no definite sense of what I wanted to make of my life or my purpose. Most likely, you're going over some of the same questions I had as a high schooler:

- What do I want to do with my life?
- Can I take what I'm good at and enjoy doing and transform it into a career?
- Will college help me spread my wings, develop my character, and lead me into a satisfying personal life?
- How can I pay for a great college experience without sabotaging my financial future with debt?

I've written this book as a helpful guide to answer these questions and give you a better understanding of how to get the most out of the college experience. Essentially, I'm writing this to my younger self—to that high school senior in my family photo albums—and relaying the knowledge I wish I would have possessed when starting my college journey all those years ago. I wholeheartedly believe the advice in this book will help you answer your questions regarding one of the most important decisions in life and teach you how to do college the right way. The main idea I want you to come away with is this: earning a degree is all about becoming your best self. College isn't just about your future; it is about your present and learning how to be the best you can be in your context. My hope is that you will come away from this book equipped to not only to be a good student, but to become *the best you.*

Before College

01

Self-Discovery

WHY DOES COLLEGE MATTER? YOU may be thinking as you read that question, *Why would the president of a university even say something like that? Isn't college an expected and really important life step?* I ask this question not to scare you or perform some trick of reverse psychology, but to get you thinking about the essence and purpose of a college experience. Most importantly, I ask so you will begin thinking about what would make a college experience worthwhile to you. Now, the college experience can be—and should be—amazing and worthwhile, but only if a student does it right. And, sadly, far too many young people find college a disappointment—over 40 percent who start never graduate.[1]

While there are many factors, I believe the most significant reason for this dropout rate is that students don't know who they are or what they want out of college. So, if you are interested in college—and I will propose that college is not right for everyone (more on that later)—I want to be sure you choose the right school and make the most of your college experience. Here's the bottom line: it's not that I believe *college* is so important, it's that *learning* is important. By placing value in learning, you will find it easy to find the perfect job, excel, and move up your career ladder. After all, that's why I'm writing this book—to help anyone who wants to set themselves up for future success.

I interact with students and their families every day, and here's one thing I've learned to be true: the most successful students are those who are *prepared.* I'm not saying you need to have *every* detail written in your planner by the time mom and dad help unload your clothes and mini fridge at your freshman dorm while interrogating your roommate. Doing college the right way means having a framework in place that guides you to the best possible results. In this book, I will hit the major topics that will provide you with a proven structure to build an amazing college experience that will benefit you for a lifetime.

The Best College Prep

Let me share a little secret: your best preparation for college isn't happening when you pick your top three schools, fill out applications, write the essays, and find out the best dining halls on campus. Before you accomplish all those critical steps, I believe an even more important task should be undertaken: *self-discovery.* You need insight into *who* you are and how you are wired before you can make a college choice. *Where* you decide to go is profoundly connected with *who you want to become.* College isn't just a campus where you escape your parents for four years and find your college football team for life. It isn't just a place you go or the classes you take; it is an integral part in your development as a person and the beginning of your lifelong journey of self-discovery.

Self-discovery requires some reflection—a skill not highly valued today in our fast-paced culture. Our society functions on lightning-fast impulses and instinctive reactions. Our media and technology actively keep us in a mode of passive consuming. This environment, which overloads us with stimuli, isn't optimal for deep reflection. And I will be the first to admit that it's hard to put down your smartphone, shut off social media, and spend some time away from your friends or favorite activities. But in order to do the careful work of self-discovery, we must create an environment conducive to deep reflection and authenticity.

You might be thinking, *Self-discovery? I thought this guy was a president at a college, not a yogi!* Let me explain what I mean by self-discovery. Because of my faith background as a Christian, I describe it as the effort to understand how our Creator designed us. God has a "divine design" for each one of us—a unique set of passions, gifts, and experiences that sets you apart from everyone else.

This is why—as an educator—I am passionate about enabling students to better understand their distinctive mix of gifts, passions, personality, and experiences so they will become more aware of how to find their place successfully in adult life. When you are able to understand your divine design—how your passions, gifts, and experiences come together in conjunction with God's wisdom—you are able to truly live. I'm talking about living a life that is meaningful and ultimately satisfying.

Life Stewardship Tip #1

Take the time to practice self-reflection. When we build reflection into our decision-making process, we find confirmation that the journey we are on is—in fact— divinely inspired and filled with possibility.

Your Divine Design

I believe important clues to understanding your divine design are found by reflecting on some patterns in your life. There are three things that I believe you must examine thoroughly to better understand your divine design: Passion, Gifts, and Wisdom. By evaluating your passions and gifts and by listening to the wisdom of parents and mentors, you can develop a clearer idea of what you want higher education to do for you.

Passion

Passion is the "juice" of your life. This is what gets you up in the mornings—besides the alarms on your phone. This is what you can do for hours and it only feels like minutes have passed. One definition I really like comes from *21 Indispensable Qualities of a Leader* by John Maxwell: "Passion is always the starting point of all achievement. Passion is the energy of our soul."

What really gets you excited? I don't mean your favorite thing to eat, the video game your mom is always telling you to stop playing, or those late-night drives with your friends. What are some meaningful, productive interests or activities that you just can't wait to pursue? What is something that you could see yourself waking up every morning and looking forward to doing?

Here are some indicators that may help you identify your true passion:

- What's really important to you—a priority above everything else?
- What causes you to change plans—to abandon your schedule?
- What do you think about a lot—the good thoughts that bring you pleasure?
- What needs to be changed in the world?
- What are your true, deeply-held values— your non-negotiables related to the most important issues of life?

If you spend some time reflecting on your answers to these questions, I believe you will better understand your passion. Now you might find yourself lost here saying, "I have no clue!" If you find yourself in this position, try asking your parents; they watched you grow up and have unique insight into what you have enjoyed doing over the years. Ask your friends, teachers, and church leaders (or anyone that knows you well) what they think you are passionate about. If you still aren't sure, the questions for Gifts and Wisdom might help that light bulb go off.

Gifts

These are those talents and personality traits that are "just you." For the most part, these qualities were built into you on the day you were born. These are the things that come relatively easy for you—maybe sports, music, art, or writing. These qualities make some school subjects much easier than others. Think about the things you excel in: Can you write a great paper in under an hour? Do you not understand your friends' constant complaints about calculus because it's not that hard for you? Do you have a million hits on *YouTube* as a child piano prodigy? Are you the therapist of your friend group and does everyone always "feel so much better" after talking with you?

As you reflect on all of these factors, do you see a pattern emerging? That is the outline of your unique divine design! If you still are not as confident as you would like to be about what your gifts or passions are, you may find it helpful to take some tests that will fill in more of the picture. One resource I have found to be helpful is the MBTI personality type test. Leaders in businesses, colleges, and churches use it to help their people better understand who they are and how they are wired. On the Internet, you can access some good free versions.

Understanding and owning your giftings is perhaps the toughest part of self-discovery, especially for young men and women. An important part of self-discovery is trying new things and taking risks; don't let fear of failure get in your way. Try things outside of your comfort zone—you might discover a talent you didn't know you had.

Wisdom

How do you combine your passion and giftings in a way that serves a purpose and makes money? You can't possibly know all the career options available to you, much less which one to pursue. As a teenager, no one would expect you to have a huge data bank of knowledge and wisdom, but hopefully you have adults around you who have wisdom they can pass on to you. Whether it's your family, teachers, coaches, pastors, or other mentors, find someone who can speak to what you're good at and offer helpful advice as to what your options are. Even talking to people to figure out what you definitely don't want to do is helpful! Listen and learn from other people's experiences—you can save yourself time and money this way.

As a teenager, nobody expects you to have it all figured out, and chances are you don't. But luckily, there are people all throughout your community who can help—people who can *mentor* you. In my life, it was my mentors who were responsible for demonstrating how my passions and gifts could be used in a career and actually helped me secure an opportunity to develop them in that field.

Do you have someone similar in your life—maybe you don't even realize that this person is already there? Is there a particular teacher that just seems to "get you"? Or maybe it's a leader of an organization you belong to? Could it be your youth leader at church? Maybe you have a great boss or older co-worker at your part-time job? You may find it a little hard to believe, but the world is full of people who want to help you. Usually, we have to take the initiative to ask for help. I know that can be scary and humbling, but the payoff is invaluable! If you have someone, take some extra time to find out what they may know about you that you may not even know about yourself. Having a mentor helps you create positive effects in every area of your life and can enable you to better understand yourself.

Life Stewardship Tip #2

If you don't have a mentor (someone who knows you well, listens to you, encourages you, wants the best for you, is honest, and offers you wise advice), think of someone you know who could be a mentor and simply ask, "Would you be my mentor?"

> *Most people love the idea of helping someone else—in particular a younger person.*

Maximizing *You*

Choosing the right school to continue your education is an important choice in what I like to call life stewardship, by which I mean the responsibility we each have to make the most out of what we have been blessed with. When you are selecting a university, you are choosing what you believe will be the best place to help you wisely steward your passions and gifts, developing them to better fulfill what you feel your life is all about. That's what an education should do: *Hit the bullseye of what you need to best advance your divine design.*

The mission statement at Southeastern University describes well what I think is so important about education. We seek, "To equip students to discover and develop their divine design so they can serve Christ and the world through spirit-empowered life, learning, and leadership."

Throughout this book, I will be explaining different facets of life stewardship (including some specific tips) that will help you get the most out of your college experience. I want to demonstrate how you can become a highly-effective steward of your life—what you are excited about and, ultimately, what you want to get paid for doing. Now that we have laid the foundation for your journey of self-discovery and how to think about what you want out of a college experience, let's get down to the nitty-gritty details of deciding where to go.

Certainly, choosing where to go to college is one of the most important decisions of your life, but many students struggle to get this right. According to research, **over a third of students will transfer to a different school**.[2] And a large portion of these transfers take place in the first or second year, which means students are unsatisfied with their school experience, end up choosing a major that isn't available at their college, or feel they will be better served by changing schools. By taking the time to explore your options and carefully choose the right college, you are making a significant investment that will greatly influence your future.

My *Do College Right* Checklist

o   Write out answers to what you believe
    are your passions and gifts.
o   Think about how you can best stew-
    ard your passions and gifts.
o   Who is someone you consider to be a
    mentor to you?
o   Take some time to reflect on your
    divine design.

Notes

02

Exploring
College Options

NOW THAT YOU HAVE A CLEARER UN-
derstanding of who you are and the direction you
are headed in your life, the next step in preparing to do college right is to start thinking about
what type of school would be the best fit for you.
Beyond picking a major, getting good grades, and
ultimately leaving college with a degree that helps
you land a good job, what are your expectations of
college life? What kind of friends do you hope to
have? Are you hoping to find someone to marry?
What will you do for fun? How about your spiritual life—do you expect it to be challenged? All
of these questions relate to the uniqueness of each
college or university community.

Every school is a wonderful fit for some students but can also be a miserable experience for others. So, it's important to learn as much as you can about the day-to-day life of students on campus and ask yourself if you would like that to be your life for the next four years. Perhaps the most important issue to evaluate is: what kind of people do you want to spend these critical college years with? What kind of environment and teachers will help you best realize your potential? What kind of lifelong friendships do you want to develop while in college?

As you evaluate the culture of schools you are considering, you need a grid that helps guide you to a quality decision—a choice that is not only based on emotions (they certainly have a role in this decision), but also on objectively comparing the cultural aspects important to you. One image I like to use to describe the college experience is a smartphone: your device provides you with the basic platform—in college that's the academics, cost, internships, post-graduate job placement, and so on. But the apps you download on your phone represent the college culture—housing options, friends, food, activities, diversity, the arts, sporting events, locale, weather, off-campus community, and much more. The apps are what make it uniquely yours. What kind of "apps" do you want on your phone for college?

Campus Culture

Every school has a unique campus culture—think of it like a collegiate fingerprint. Whether you live on campus or off, are part time or full time, you will be spending the majority of the next four years around the faculty, students, and campus of your university. The culture these individuals and the environment create really matters, so before selecting a school you need to carefully consider the elements of daily life that are important to you. It's not only a matter of finding a school with the right academic program—you want to choose the right school with an atmosphere that will best usher you into this next exciting phase of life. Here are some questions to consider:

- How much emphasis does the school place on life outside of the classroom, and how will that impact you?
- Are you looking for a school that protects, encourages, and promotes diversity?
- Do you place an emphasis on an outdoor lifestyle, intramural sports, or general physical fitness?
- Is worldview an important factor? Do you want significant opportunities to connect with others who share your faith at a university?

- Do you welcome the more challenging environment of a secular university where your faith might be significantly tested and strengthened?
- If you choose to be a commuter student, how accessible are the school's resources to you? Are there opportunities to connect to others in the commuter community?

Christian vs. Secular College

Whether or not the differences between a secular and Christian campus will impact you is an individual matter. Many Christians attend non-religious universities due to lower tuition costs or access to academic opportunities and come out thriving. Thanks to campus ministries, finding an opportunity to explore and profess your faith is not just limited to Christian schools.

Since I'm the president of a Christian university, I do want to share my insights on the question of what type of school may be best for you in regard to your faith. A Christian college isn't just for ministry majors anymore—many schools now offer full liberal arts programs, business degrees, or trade programs. And if you are interested in working within a ministry or parachurch field, Christian colleges still offer holistic programs of academic, relational, and spiritual training. Non-Christian colleges, on the other hand, may offer ministry-adjacent programs that can give you a better variety of post-college careers in the traditional workplace.

The Christian collegiate community is diverse— no two Christian colleges are exactly alike—and more likely to offer plentiful opportunities to explore and deepen your spiritual life than a secular university. Even better, a shared faith foundation can help you develop meaningful relationships with other believers, making it less intimidating and even easier to begin those new college friendships. A non-Christian college may also have faith groups or organizations you can join, but they won't all be Christian. You'll find people and community groups of all different faiths, shapes, and sizes at most secular universities. However, if you find a group of students who come from a similar life and church background, your bond may grow deeper and tighter as you face secular college life together.

Life Stewardship Tip #3

No matter what type of college you attend—Christian or secular—be sure to develop at least one or two close friends who share your spiritual values.

Christian college rules vary, but most will have general guidelines regarding curfews, alcohol and drugs, on-campus or off-campus activities, and social behavior. Some students may scoff at such rules, but the guidelines do help provide a safe atmosphere with healthy boundaries that will assist in one's transition from home to college to career. Whereas at secular universities, it's up to the student to put boundaries around their college lifestyle.

I am very proud of how much effort we devote to providing a wholesome yet stimulating faith environment at Southeastern University (SEU). Here is how we describe the experience for students:

> Campus life is marked by a culture of discipleship where students are challenged to excel academically, socially, and spiritually. Both in and out of the classroom, students are empowered to become lifelong learners. Through mentoring opportunities, they discover their leadership capacity to live life committed to serving Christ globally. Through innovative chapel services, intramurals, and more than eighteen varsity sports, the Southeastern "college experience" is second to none.

SEU students create memories and friendships that last a lifetime.[3]

Collegiate True or False

*It will be quite difficult to maintain my faith if
I attend a large state university.
[Answered at the end of the chapter.]*

Campus Safety

When you are thinking about a good campus cultural fit for yourself, the issue of campus safety may not immediately come to mind. But, believe me, you will not fully enjoy your college experience if you don't feel secure.

In our current society, safety is a bigger issue than ever before. Sadly, in 2018, there were twenty-four school shootings in the United States.[4] That's a terrifying number and speaks to a reality which certainly didn't exist during my high school and college years. While most of these tragedies occurred at primary and secondary schools, the college campus was not immune. Another prevalent and troubling issue on college campuses is the increasing number of forcible sexual offenses.

Colleges are working very hard to increase

campus security, I can assure you. But I still recommend that you research the safety of the colleges on your list. There are many resources available to help you determine the safety of your potential schools, but one of my favorites is offered by the government. The U.S. Department of Education provides an online resource for researching campus crimes by school over the past three years.[5] If you're considering several universities, the website even allows you to do a side-by-side safety comparison of up to four schools.

Campus visits can also help give you an overall feel of the safety of a university. When you visit, keep an eye out for how well pathways are lit (imagine walking across campus after an evening class), observe how many emergency stations are along campus walkways, and ask the prospective school to give you a rundown of their campus safety procedures and programs.

The Campus Visit

The best way to learn about the culture of any college is to spend some time there and take a guided tour. Today, colleges offer several opportunities during the academic year to spend one to two days on campus visiting with admissions counselors, touring facilities, eating cafeteria meals, meeting students and faculty, visiting classes, and attending sporting or other events. There may even be the option of spending a night in a campus dormitory. Take your "Culture Checklist" (see Appendix) with you to each college and create a detailed report of what you find—and how comfortable you feel—at each school. Here are some important questions to think about as you visit colleges and will be reflected in your Culture Checklist:

- What type of environment will encourage you to grow more as a person?
- To what extent will your specific interests in non-academic areas like sports or artistic events affect your college choice?
- Do you think a larger, more impersonal campus would be pleasing—or do you want a smaller college where it may be easier to connect personally with more people?
- Would you like to go to college in a big city or in a smaller college town?

These visits will wear you out, so be sure you are well rested before you arrive. Also, dress casually and wear comfortable shoes—you will walk a lot! And since one or both of your parents will probably be with you, remember to have a good attitude toward them and their needs on these visits. After all, this is stressful for them—they are evaluating numerous issues like the college's reputation, cost, safety, fit for you, and more. Enjoy this experience as a team!

The on-campus visits will probably solidify your top choice for the college you want to attend. This is a wonderful moment in your life—enjoy every second. And fill in your checklist as it will help you remember things you may forget in the aftermath of your stimulating campus visit.

I realize that you may not be able to visit some of the schools on your list. Do not despair! With today's technology, you can find out a great deal about campus culture by doing research online. Many colleges now offer digital tours, where you can see the entire campus from the comfort of your couch. Here are some research tips if you can't physically visit the college:

- Totally comb through every part of the college's website. Be sure to take the virtual tours and watch other videos.
- Contact the college admissions office and obtain brochures and other printed resources.
- Learn if these colleges will have representatives at a local college fair.
- Follow the school on social media. Download college/student apps.
- Check out local, state, and regional websites to learn about the broader culture of

where this college is located.

- If available, watch college sporting and cultural events online.
- Call and talk with an admissions representative about any lingering questions you have.
- If you are interested in specific campus organizations or clubs, contact the student leaders of these groups.
- Find out if any current students are from your hometown. Meet one or more of them when they are home on a break. Take them for a cup of coffee to learn more about life on campus. You might also be able to do this with college alumni who live in your area.

You can actually learn a lot without making a campus visit. In fact, even if you are able to experience the campus in person, gathering information through the above activities is also a good idea for you—a one-day or two-day visit will be exciting but also somewhat overwhelming, and you won't learn or retain everything.

Here are the most important things to remember: First, as with so many other factors in your college decision, the better you know yourself and what will fulfill you, the more likely you will make a superb choice. Second, don't discount the value of the culture you will find yourself in on a daily basis.

My *Do College Right* Checklist

- o Besides academics, what are the three most important things you want from your college experience?
- o What do you think would be best for you: a Christian or secular college?
- o Where do you think you might do the best academically: a smaller or larger school? Or will it not matter to you?

Collegiate True or False

False. Securing what you believe is really up to you—and your faith probably will be challenged in certain ways no matter where you attend college. It is probably true to say that you are more likely to find more aggressive testing of your faith at a secular institution—public or private. But no matter where you go, it will be up to you to find strong fellow believers who will stand with you as you make your faith "more your own."

03

The ROI Factor

THE ROI ("RETURN ON INVESTMENT" for all the non-future business majors) for college is an important consideration as you are looking at what school to attend. More and more students and their families are concluding that a college education is just too expensive. This conclusion is understandable, because at the time I'm writing this (2019), student loan debt in the U.S. is over $1.5 trillion—that's more than either the credit card debt or auto loan debt of all Americans. The average graduating student's loan debt is now $37,172[6] and some predictions put the default rate on student loans at nearly 40 percent by 2023![7] And with the current cost of tuition and room and board at public universities averaging $21,370 per year and

$48,510 per year at private non-profit universities, loan debt for students enrolling shows no signs of slowing down.[8]

As a college president, I could not be more passionate about the value of post high school learning and career preparation, but I also believe higher education in America has to change. We should not think that something as valuable as a college education will ever be free, but I maintain that it's up to colleges and universities—not the taxpayers—to figure out how to make what these institutions offer as accessible and affordable to as many qualified students as possible. College is still a very worthwhile investment, because a college education will not only benefit you intellectually and socially, but it will also increase your value in today's increasingly competitive job environment.

You might be under the impression that you really have no alternative but to go deep into debt while pursuing a college degree. Fortunately, there is something of a revolution brewing in how colleges and universities are responding to the issue of accessibility and affordability in higher education. Those of us who believe that education is still the best investment anyone can make in improving the opportunity to succeed in life are working to make sure you get the greatest ROI out of college.

As much as we can hope for and work towards a better future, you still have to deal with the current reality: college is expensive. However, there are ways you can finance the education you need at a price that makes sense. I will explain in this chapter and the chapters to come how you can pursue higher education without accruing a large amount of debt.

Maximizing ROI

Perhaps you already have learned more about ROI by watching *The Social Network* or from binge-watching *Shark Tank*. In either case, you don't have to be Mark Zuckerberg or Mark Cuban to ensure you make smart choices with your time and money. Evaluating the ROI of particular colleges is an important step in making the right college choice.

Determining how much a degree program will cost, compared to the earning potential of your intended degree, is the way to establish the ROI of different schools. While it's true that the potential future salary for students who earn a bachelor's degree varies by major, according to the U.S. Bureau of Labor Statistics, the average annual salary for a college graduate with a bachelor's degree was $59,124, while a high school graduate could expect an average income of $35,256 per year.[9] Statistically, getting any degree is definitely financially beneficial.

So, what might your salary be when you graduate? You can find out on the Internet. For example,
payscale.com provides a quick view of average salary potential by degree,[10] while other websites like
salary.com can help you determine how much you
should make based on job type and location.

Your salary might be great after you graduate, but does your university succeed at placing
its graduates in their chosen fields? Nothing quite
says ROI like a school whose students are highly
employable after graduation! Thanks to the *Princ-
eton Review,* discovering how well a school ranks
in the area of job placement is easier than ever.
Their annual report, "Best College Values," ranks
the top twenty-five schools according to their career services and the median starting salary and
mid-career salary of alumni. If none of those
schools happen to be on your short list, there are
other ways to evaluate how well a university ranks
in the area of job placement, like asking the office of admissions. I suggest—with the colleges or
universities you are considering—that you find out
how successful their graduates are in finding jobs
in your future career field.

Sometimes it isn't as much about the ratings
as it is the resources available to students. Many
schools offer job fairs, networking opportunities,
resume and interview prep, and even online career and internship portals. Don't be afraid to ask

questions about your prospective school's career services and career placement programs.

After you learn more about how much you can make after college, it's time to compare that to the cost of your degree program. Most schools make tuition costs and financial aid information readily available on their websites. Another great resource is the Consumer Financial Protection Bureau, which offers cost comparisons for different schools (think *trivago.com* but for universities).[11] After comparing those numbers, does college make more sense for you?

Still, as important as ROI is, be sure you choose a school with a learning environment that will inspire personal growth, nudge you outside of your comfort zone, and encourage you to try and pursue new things. The college experience will lead you to discover your highest potential. You are, after all, your greatest investment, and discovering what you want to do in life is the greatest return.

Collegiate True or False

Even though college students normally do not have any steady income, it is easy for them to obtain credit cards.
[Answered at the end of the chapter.]

Different Paths

You are aware by now what a huge proponent I am of education, but I am a realist too: not everyone wants to—or should want to—pursue a traditional four-year degree. What is important is getting the necessary education that will set you up for a satisfying career and reasonable standard of living.

Recently, the CEO of Apple, Tim Cook, publicly stated that, in many cases within the field of technology, a "tech degree" is not necessary. At an American Workforce Policy Advisor meeting, Cook noted that nearly 50 percent of the people the company hired in the U.S. in 2018 did not have a four-year degree. He also stated that he strongly believes that computer coding proficiency should be a requirement for all high school students graduating in the U.S.[12]

Another prominent corporate executive, IBM CEO, Ginni Rometty, recently coined the term "new-collar jobs" as a way of describing valuable tech-based jobs (for example, cloud-computing technician) that will not require a four-year or higher college degree.[13]

Frankly, often a well-planned undergraduate program—made possible by a college committed to delivering high value—can be completed in less than four years. Higher education increasingly is not so much credit-hours oriented as outcome oriented. In other words, you should have more flexibility in a degree program. For example, you learn that in your desired future job good writing skills are essential. But to have such skills, you may not need three writing courses taken over a two-year span. You might be able to acquire an adequate writing skill set in one yearlong course, which would allow you to finish in less than four years. So, if you are not totally convinced that a traditional four-year college degree is right for you, how else might you continue your education? Let me suggest a few options other than a four-year degree that might interest you:

- Associate degree from a community college
- Certificate from a college
- Online degree or local university extension
- Trade or tech school
- Apprenticeship
- Gap year
- Military

• • •

Whether you finish college in four or two years, attend a trade school, or learn online while you work a part-time job, remember this: *The best ROI depends on obtaining the appropriate education related to your career field.* Are you going to get a quality education at a cost that provides high value for the long term?

ROI is a meaningful and strategic means for thinking about your education. Of course, being an avid learner is always a good idea, but shouldn't we be smart in how much we spend to obtain a good education? Makes sense to me. In fact, it makes a lot of cents—and dollars, too (pardon the pun)!

My *Do College Right* Checklist

- Discuss the ROI of a college degree with your parents.
- Considering the type of career you would like to pursue, what might your starting salary be when you graduate?
- How might student loan debt restrict your housing choices after college, especially where you might like to work and live?

Collegiate True or False

True. College students receive frequent offers to apply for credit cards. Don't fall for them! It's better to have a debit card tied to a bank account that you use sparingly or only in emergencies. And it might be wise to have this be a joint account with a parent who will be able to monitor your spending and provide accountability. Don't despair—you will have many years after college to handle all of your finances on your own!

04

Deciding Where to Go

AFTER EVALUATING COLLEGE
culture and where you might find the best return on
investment (ROI), the time has come to begin your
serious investigation of specific colleges. This could
become an intimidating task since there are nearly 5,000 two-year and four-year accredited colleges
and universities in the United States but, thankfully,
you just need to find the right one for you![14]

To be sure, a number of factors will reduce the
college pool for you—issues like your grade point
average, finances, distance you can travel, and
more. Still, you should begin the process with an
open mind. For example, you may find a school
that you think is just perfect, but the cost is way
beyond your budget. Don't cross it off the list until

you at least learn what kind of scholarships and other financial aid are available (I'll discuss finances in greater depth in chapters 5 and 6).

When I began my college journey, I was already working part time at a job that I believed was related to my long-term career interests. So, attending the local community college made sense. I also knew that no matter where I went to college, I would have to take some basic courses like English Composition and Speech, so I signed up for such courses. Later, as my career objectives sharpened, I put more research into determining what would be the right college fit for me.

As you might anticipate, I have a plan for you to consider:

1. Determine your major
2. Obtain information on colleges
3. Narrow the field
4. Talk to your parents or guardians
5. Make contact with schools and visit
6. Submit applications on time

Determine Your Major

If you are one hundred percent certain that you know what you want to do and how to make a living after college, this first step will be simple. But if you are like most people, you may not know yet what career path to follow. You have passions and gifts, but aren't ready to decide on "the one." There's nothing wrong with that—many your age are in the same boat. But I encourage you to at least narrow the broad direction you want to head.

For example, if you know you want to work with computers and/or related technology, then you will be able to better navigate your college course choices as your specific interests solidify. But if you have interest in both computers and veterinary medicine, you need to explore some ways to help you choose between the two so you will select the right major and university. As we've already discussed, the price of a college education is soaring exponentially these days, so flipping from major to major could leave you with massive student loan debt—impinging on your life for years or even decades to come. I know of a student who spent three years preparing to enter medical school, then decided she wanted to pursue gender studies. That radical change in direction meant spending another three years in college—and amassing three more years of student loan debt. Plus, after getting her degree, she had quite limited job opportunities due to the major she pursued.

I know it may seem hard—maybe close to impossible—to choose a major, but the effort is so worth it! So how can you narrow your choice, avoid several major switches, save a lot of money, and perhaps even prevent yourself from ending up in a job you hate after college? Here are some ideas:

- **Ask yourself, "What am I naturally good at?"** There are no right answers, so list everything you can think of—big and small. You might answer, "I'm really good at keeping my room clean!" That quality may seem insignificant, but it's a trait that reveals you are organized, disciplined, and good at time management. (You might excel as a teacher!) The better you understand certain trends in your life that reveal what you're good at, the easier it should be to narrow your choices on a major. Your core qualities and your ability to adapt are what will really matter. I have experienced this myself, drawing on personal abilities during my time as a sports broadcaster, pastor, and university president.
- **List five majors.** Three majors should be what you think you want to do, and the other two should be majors that could interest you.
- **Do some research on your own.** Research possible careers related to the majors you are considering. Check out the potential income in each career option. Beyond

that, what's the outlook for job availability, the job satisfaction of those in the field, and even the opportunity to select a desired geographic location where you would like to work and live?

- **Shadow someone in that line of work.** This will take some effort, but try to spend more than a few hours actually observing someone doing the work. Ideally, do this for all five majors you have listed. I think you may be surprised at what you learn.

- **Sit down with a parent or a trusted mentor.** Bring the information you've gathered and meet with someone you trust, a person who will help you objectively look at your research and help you shape a decision.

Once you have completed these tasks, you will be quite certain about or close to determining your perfect major (or at least you will have eliminated several options). And if you still are not quite sure—*it might happen*—you certainly can change your major in college. That won't be the end of the world—believe me, it happens a lot (see chapter 10). The important thing is to end up in a career that matches your interests and abilities—that's how you will succeed and be satisfied.

Obtain Information

Now that you have direction on what you want to study, it's time to identify several schools that are known for high-quality training in those majors. The more specific or narrow your choice of a major, the more research that may be required to identify the right school(s). On the other hand, if you want to major, for instance, in computer science or become an elementary school teacher, you will find many colleges offering those majors.

Of course, your information search can begin on your computer—colleges now have extensive information available through their websites. Be sure to create some digital or paper files where you can store your findings as you narrow your choices.

Narrow the Field

As you gather information, keep in mind the important issue of location. No, not everyone can attend a college that's on the beach or in the mountains, but you can dream, can't you? What's important to realize is that where your college is located might be just as crucial as considering where your first job might be located. In fact, one may very well determine the other.

A recent discussion paper from the Institute of Labor Economics indicated that new companies are several times more likely to recruit from their local universities within the first few years of opening a new location. What this means is that considering the business and job potential in the vicinity of your college of choice is more important than ever.

Aside from how your school's location will affect your future, it is also helpful to consider how it will affect the next four years of your life. Here are some things to consider:

- How close to home, family, and old friends do you want to be? Or do you like the idea of a new beginning?
- What kind of weather and environment would you prefer? If skiing or snowboarding is your thing, then Florida may not be your best choice (although I think Florida is amazing—are you sure you might not like spending time at the beach?).
- Do you prefer nights at the theater or long hikes?
- Would you prefer to live in a big city or a college town?

Even if family proximity, weather, outdoor activities, or access to urban amenities are not on your list of essentials, at least consider a school's location in conjunction with your career goals. Studying film production in Los Angeles or music business in Nashville could provide access to a multitude of internships, connections, and job opportunities.

Talk to Your Parents or Guardians

Okay, you have done a lot of work to clarify your choices for a major and an ideal college or two—congratulations on a job well done! But now it's time to present your findings and wishes to some important people in your life—your parents, guardians, or others helping you make a decision. After all, in most cases, they have a significant stake in this because they will be contributing money, time, and other resources to supporting you in this big step.

When explaining your choice of college to your parents, stick to topics like academics, culture, and cost. It certainly is not wrong that you might want to go to school with your old friends or with a boyfriend or girlfriend—but your decision must involve many other critical factors. So here are some helpful hints on how best to present your college choice to your parents:

Consider the Potential Obstacles

Do your parents already have a college in mind for you? Maybe it's the college everyone in the

family has attended for generations. This could be
difficult but assure your parents that, as much as
you appreciate the "good ole family U," it doesn't
provide you with the best training for *your* ultimate
success. Or maybe the favored family college has
become super expensive—and it will be your college loans to repay.

Explain Your Research

Show your parents that you've done your homework on choosing a major and finding the best college matches for your ultimate success. Your desire
to do this right will mean so much to them. Show
them the facts by comparing your choices to other options. Many times, when you do a side-by-
side comparison, the choice becomes very clear to
everyone. Your parents will appreciate your effort
and logic in reaching a conclusion.

Interject Your Personality

Because of who you are, you may have found a connection growing to the school options you are considering. Your parents want what's best for you—
they want you to enjoy college, not be miserable. So,
a good fit is so important. Your parents will respect
your efforts to consider your personal needs, too,
and not just academics in selecting a university.

College is a time to grow, learn, and explore—
it's scary *and* exciting, but remember that your

parents are your biggest fans and they want your success too. After you've presented your decision to them, listen to their thoughts and have a good discussion. If they completely disagree with your choice(s), take a deep breath, and calmly ask them to explain their reasons. They may see obstacles or opportunities that you missed while on your decision-making journey—listen carefully and calmly.

Regardless, this decision-making process doesn't have to be negative—it can be a very positive and exciting experience for you and your parents! And if you have three potential schools in mind, hopefully as you all work through this together, you will eventually reach a consensus on the one that seems a perfect match!

Make Contact and Visit

Now that you have done the research on your major, obtained information, narrowed the field, and—hopefully—have your parents on board, it's time to schedule some more personal discussion with representatives of the school(s) you've selected. Perhaps one or even all of your choices will be participating in a college fair near where you live—that's an excellent opportunity to meet representatives and learn more about each school. Or you can schedule telephone calls or even Skype sessions. Whenever possible, of course, include your parents in these opportunities.

Finally, if at all possible, schedule an in-person visit to the campuses—ideally on a preview weekend. And, as mentioned before, if you are unable to schedule a visit in person, learn as much as you can about the campus online via virtual video and other resources.

Collegiate True or False

It's better to make an unannounced visit to a campus since then you can learn what the real "vibe" is, rather than what the school wants you to think during a "preview event."
[Answered at the end of the chapter.]

Submit Applications on Time

Should you apply before or after your on-campus visit? I don't think there's one right answer to that question. Obviously, if your college choices are in state, or not that far away from where you live, then it might make more sense to visit the campuses before you submit applications. You may find after the visits that you are not interested in one or more of your initial favorites, which may mean you have more investigative work to do. If one or more of your chosen schools are some distance away, then you may want to postpone a visit until you learn whether you are accepted or not. How you decide is up to you and your parents.

My biggest advice on the issue of applications is don't procrastinate! After all the work you've done to narrow your choice(s), don't reduce your chances for acceptance and financial aid by waiting too long to apply. Applications for admission are accepted as early as twelve months before the requested entry semester for most schools. Regardless of how you navigate the application process, make sure you meet the critical deadlines. Here's what they look like at the time this book was written. (To make sure you are on schedule, consult the specific application requirements at each school.)

- Fall (a year prior to entry): Take the ACT or SAT, apply for scholarships, schedule college campus tours.
- October 1: FAFSA (Free Application for Federal Student Aid) filing opens for the next academic school year. Be sure to submit yours as close to this date as possible to get priority as funds are first come, first served.
- November 1: Normally the application

deadline for incoming students for the up-coming spring semester.

- Spring: Retake the ACT or SAT if needed, complete scholarship applications.
- May 1: Normally the application deadline for incoming students for the fall semester.
- June 1: Deadline to file a FAFSA form (depending on your state).
- Summer: Complete the financial aid process, attend orientation, and review your class schedule.

• • •

Now that you have done all the hard work of choosing a college, the next step is to determine more specifically how to pay for your education. Let's find out in the next chapter.

My *Do College Right* Checklist

- Talk to your high school guidance counselor early in your junior year. Discuss your college goals. Verify with your counselor that you are on track with your college prep courses.
- Starting your junior year of high school, spend at least an hour a week doing research on colleges.
- Make sure your parents feel very included in your evaluation of colleges and your final choice(s).
- Prepare a calendar of important deadlines related to college applications. Ask a parent to help you monitor this.

Collegiate True or False

False. If you just drop in, you will probably miss out on opportunities. If you spend one or more days on campus, follow your Campus Visit Culture Checklist (see Appendix), and talk to students randomly, you will have ample opportunity to determine the "vibe."

05

The Cost of College

THERE'S NO AVOIDING THE REALITY that the basic cost of a college degree can be a massive burden for budget-minded families. My central desire for you—if you really want to secure a college degree—is that you find a way to achieve that goal without breaking the bank.

Each year in the United States, **approximately $49 billion is gifted to students like you in the form of scholarships and grants**.[15] That is 49 billion reasons to learn the ins and outs of the scholarship process and how to grab hold of some much-needed financial aid. Scholarships and grants come from several different sources, including the federal government, your state, your college, and even private organizations. In the 2016-2017 academic school year, some **$2.3 billion in federal grant money was left unclaimed due to one significant factor: students didn't fill out their FAFSA** (Free Application for Federal Student Aid).[16]

That's billions of dollars of free money that wasn't used. Billions. I want to make sure that doesn't happen to you, because the opportunities for financial aid are everywhere. In chapter 6, I'll help walk you through the process—from understanding types of scholarships to mastering filling out the application so you secure the financial aid available. Your mission is, should you choose to accept it, *no scholarship left behind!* Before we dive headfirst into scholarships though, it is important for you to understand the language and processes of financial aid.

Financial Aid Terms and Definitions

In order to avoid student debt, it's important to understand what types of aid are available to you. Financial aid for college—or any post-secondary education—comes in many different forms and from many different sources. Distinguishing between loans and grants, grants and scholarships, and government aid and private loans will help

Collegiate True or False

*Only public, state universities
require the FAFSA.
[Answered at the end of the chapter.]*

Loans

Loans must be paid back (usually with interest) and can come from both the government and private loan providers (banks and credit unions). Government loans, for instance, tend to come with lower interest rates and more lenient repayment options than private loans. In fact, government loans are often offered as part of the financial aid package provided by your university.

Grants

Grants and scholarships are often referred to as "gift aid" and are provided without the expectation of repayment. The two words are sometimes used synonymously, but there is a helpful distinction.

Grants are typically need-based—money designated to students who have a financial need, often determined by a family's income level.

Scholarships, on the other hand, are most often merit-based: they are given to students who demonstrate an academic, athletic, artistic, or even social achievement.

Scholarships

Scholarships can be further broken down into the following categories:

- *External scholarships*: Financial aid offered by private or non-profit organizations.
- *School-sponsored scholarships*: Need-based, academic, and athletic scholarships offered by your university.
- *Need-based scholarships*: Grants offered by the government as well as private organizations and schools. These can be determined by your financial situation, but also can include scholarships for underrepresented groups, first generation college students, and other non-academic factors.
- *Merit-based scholarships*: Based on GPA, test scores (PSAT, SAT, and ACT), athletics, artistic ability, and more.
- *Renewable scholarships*: Gift aid that can be renewed each academic year, sometimes contingent on grades and enrollment.
- *Non-renewable scholarships*: One-time gift aid given for a single academic year or semester.

Now that you know what types of scholarships and grants are available, it is important to understand how you qualify for the different types of aid, which brings us to the FAFSA. The **F**ree **A**pplication for **F**ederal **S**tudent **A**id is one of the first things you will want to fill out with the help of your parents—even prior to choosing your university.

The FAFSA helps colleges and the government determine if you are eligible for certain need-based grants and loans. The FAFSA application, which should be submitted each year you are in college, uses tax information, income, and family size, among other things, to determine the expected family contribution (EFC) toward your college tuition. Once the EFC is calculated, the government and your school can offer financial aid that helps supplement scholarships and other aid you may receive. Remember that $2.3 billion left on the table a few years back? There's free financial aid available, and all it requires is the time it takes to fill out the FAFSA!

Public vs. Private

In most instances, it costs less to attend a state school in your state of residence where you should find more in-state discounts, financial aid, and scholarships. Whichever path you take—in or out of state—the other kinds of scholarships previously discussed should still apply.

Since I am president of a private Christian institution, my emphasis in this book is on that type of college. Of course, most Christian colleges are private—while they typically exhibit a high standard of academic performance, they may also come with a hefty price tag. But don't fear! Many churches and Christian organizations sponsor grants and scholarships for students like you. Some Christian colleges even forego or reduce tuition rates for the benefit of those considering Christian ministry.

While both Christian and non-Christian colleges can provide you with community, high academic standards, and valuable non-academic experiences, schools with a culture built on the ethos of your faith may naturally align with your values *and* your life goals.

• • •

Determining how to pay for a college education is a demanding, often frustrating process for both you and your parents. Work as a team, stay patient with each other, remember this will take some time. You will find the money to do this and you

will always be glad you did. The next step may
be the most important of all: start looking for any
gift aid you can find. I'll show you how in the next
chapter.

My *Do College Right* Checklist

- o In your own words, explain the difference between a loan and a grant.
- o Start working on your FAFSA as soon as possible. It requires significant parental involvement so don't procrastinate!

Collegiate True or False

False. Virtually all colleges and universities use the FAFSA to determine how much financial aid will be granted to a student—regardless of family income. The FAFSA is critically important to obtaining as much aid as possible—submit it early every year!

06

Scholarships

THESE DAYS, COLLEGE REQUIRES SUCH a significant investment—and most students end up borrowing money to help finance their education. Your goal should be to keep student loan debt as low as possible. One way to do that is with financial gift aid or scholarships. The possibility of helping pay for a college education with scholarships is so important that I'm devoting an entire chapter to the topic. For various reasons, you may be thinking, *I won't qualify for scholarships anyway, so why bother?* Wait a minute! You may have bought into some myths about college scholarships. Let's set the record straight.

Myths are plentiful when it comes to college scholarships, so let's take them down now:

- **Myth: You have to have great grades or be an athlete.** Of course, it's always a good idea to have the best grades possible, and being a great athlete may result in an athletic scholarship, but many scholarships are based on financial need or a wide variety of other factors.
- **Myth: You have to be a minority student.** Wrong. Many, many other qualities will qualify you for scholarships.
- **Myth: You have to come from a low-income family.** Financial aid is often tied to a student's family resources, but many scholarships are awarded for a student's interests, experiences, and aptitudes.
- **Myth: Thousands of students apply for scholarships—I have no chance.** Yes, this is a highly competitive adventure. But with the right strategy and dedicated time and effort (explained fully in this chapter), you can win!
- **Myth: Small award scholarships are not worth the effort.** This one is devastating—maybe the worst scholarship myth.

Do not believe it. Consider this: Generally speaking, fewer students apply for smaller award scholarships. So, let's say you spend 40 hours applying for scholarships and only win one that will give you $250 a year for your four years of college. That's $1000 divided by 40—$25 an hour! Not a bad "wage" if you are making $8 an hour at a fast food job! And that's also $1000 that you won't have to pay back from a student loan. Nothing small about that!

- **Myth: You have to wait until your senior year to apply.** Don't wait to apply! As with selecting a college and submitting applications, deadlines have moved up for many scholarships. Plan to start considering scholarship options and submitting applications during your junior year of high school. And don't forget to keep applying for scholarships every year while in college.
- **Myth: You have to be an incredible writer to win.** Nope. Again, writing well is always a good idea, but many scholarships are awarded on how well you follow instructions and your creativity in addressing the essay topic—not on your ability to be the next Ernest Hemingway!
- **Myth: If I win a scholarship, I'll lose other financial aid.** There's some

truth to this myth—colleges vary on how this issue is handled. Find out what your college's policy is. But please remember: a gift (scholarship) is always preferred to a loan, because you don't have to pay the gift giver back!

Those are some of the scholarship myths and there are more I didn't mention. But here's what you really need to know: with a good strategy and work, you can win a scholarship. So, don't skip this chapter and please read on.

Building Your Scholarship Strategy

Obtaining scholarships is a lot of work, which is why if you treat the application process as a part-time job, you increase your chances of success. Many students grow quite weary of the work required and give up, which means more opportunity for those who stay at it. But I don't want to sugarcoat this for you, finding scholarships is time-consuming and exhausting. Think of it this way, the harder you work to find scholarships, the more money you will make after you graduate since you will have less debt to pay off.

The better job you do of understanding the scholarship process before you begin, the better the

outcome will be. So here are some suggestions on
how to develop your scholarship strategy and understand this demanding but also very rewarding
process.

Consider Your Uniqueness

What sets you apart from others? Make a master
list of all the scholarship criteria that pertain to you:

- Talents
- Achievements (academic, artistic, athletic,
  and extra-curricular)
- Underrepresentation (gender, ethnicity, lo-
  cation, first generation)
- Hobbies
- Volunteer work
- Religious affiliation

Explore Locally

Are there any seminars being held in your area
that discuss how to acquire scholarships? This may
be something your high school is sponsoring. Go to
any event that might help you; however, *avoid events
or websites where you will be asked to pay for help with the
scholarship process.*

Some smaller businesses and clubs in your community have funds set up specifically for scholarships. Also, consider corporations in your area.
Businesses often will provide scholarships for chil-

dren of their employees or even for associates or suppliers. You just need to keep your eyes and ears open—then apply.

Every college has scholarships—there might be some that are major-specific, based on region, or ethnicity, etc. Look on the college website or become familiar with admissions counselors who you can ask for help to navigate the process for your maximum benefit.

Life Stewardship Tip #4

No matter how hard you try, there is no possible way to get more than twenty-four hours out of a day. This means you need to plan how to use your time but also accept that you are human and leave for tomorrow the things you did not accomplish today.

Apply for as Many Scholarships as You Can

Commit to applying for twenty scholarships a week. Yes, you read that right, *twenty!* I know, that's a lot and this is not exactly fun work. But neither is bearing the burden of student loans for decades after you graduate.

Remember, this is like a part-time job, and the

more you apply, the higher your chances of securing more college funding. Also, as I've already suggested, don't get hung up only applying for large scholarships, which are highly competitive. Smaller scholarships add up quickly and are easier to secure. I recommend applying for at least eighty scholarships (the more the merrier!).

Keep Good Records

Finally, one important key to all of this is organization: keep a spreadsheet with the name of each scholarship, requirements (for example, essay and letter of recommendation), details (address/website/email), date you applied, amount, and the potential award date.

Finding the Right Scholarships

Before the Internet, searching for the right scholarships was a real chore. There were some guidebooks and, of course, each college had a list of their scholarships. But beyond that, hunting down scholarships required exhaustive letter writing, phone calls, and—of course—some good fortune.

Thankfully, searching for scholarships has been made easier because of online scholarship databases and search engines. Now, not only can you easily search for any scholarship, you can narrow your search down to the best scholarships—the ones that would benefit you the most and the ones you have a good opportunity to win.

Even though these tools are incredibly helpful, you do need a plan so that you will maximize your time and energy in the scholarship search. Here are some tips for building and activating your plan.

Get Organized

Keep separate lists of scholarships you've already won, those you've applied for, and those you are considering. If most of your scholarships require essays, keep your essays organized by topic so you can recycle them for future applications and save valuable time that could be spent looking for more money. Keep a running total of scholarship dollars you have earned so far—as well as your financial target—so that you have a clear goal in mind.

If you are a staunch believer in writing by hand, grab a notebook, pen, and a pile of sticky notes, and you will be on your way to mastering the abundance of scholarship data. However, if the digital world is more your M.O., free tools such as Trello (*trello.com*) or Evernote (*evernote.com*) are a great way to track your scholarships and keep that information handy on your smartphone and computer at the same time. Trello even allows you to create boards, color-code your lists, and create sub-lists, so it's almost like using a real sticky note.

Don't forget the all-too-useful Google Apps. If
you aren't familiar, now might be a good time to create a free email account specifically for scholarship
applications. That way your emails, calendar, and
notes regarding this college application process are
all in one place. Use your calendar to track deadlines and set reminders so you don't miss an opportunity. There are few pains worse than preparing for
an amazing scholarship with essays and letters of
recommendation, only to miss the deadline—and
your parents won't let you hear the end of it!

Surf the Web

Start by doing a quick survey of some of the key
scholarship search engines available to you. These
include websites such as *goodcall.com*, *scholarships.
com*, and *fastweb.com*. Several of these sites even use
your profile to help match you to the right scholarships—saving you time and energy.

One thing the top search tools all have in common is the ability to filter your results, which is a
vital part of your process: *focus your search*. There
are millions of scholarships available, some are
one-off awards, and others grant significant sums
that will carry you through four years of your undergraduate education. Regardless of how big or
small the scholarship, it is important to focus your
attention on gift aid that you are most likely to win.
What skills or achievements qualify you for differ-

ent scholarships?

These factors should help you narrow your scholarship search. Use your list to identify keywords for filtering. Keep this list handy whenever you browse the web for scholarships and keep adding to it when you think of another activity or skill set that might qualify you for financial aid.

Make Lists

Based on the scholarship information you already have, make several lists. The A list would include types of scholarships you feel are easy hits (such as, academic if you have good grades). Your B list would include scholarships that have more stringent criteria (such as, an application fee and essay). Your C list might include longer shots or the out-of-the-box ones (see below). This list will make your scholarship application process a breeze!

Think Outside the Box

This tip is actually a good one to apply to just about everything in your life. However, it can be especially helpful while sharpening your scholarship hunting skills. What's outside the box regarding scholarships? Obviously I'm not talking here about broad scholarships that are tied almost exclusively to test scores and GPA. Outside the box scholarships are often awarded for creativity. For example, you could win a scholarship based on your zombie apocalypse survival skills or your ability to build a prom outfit out of duct tape.

When you get tired of browsing the web and building duct tape dresses, be sure to use the other resources available to you:

- Your school or public library's reference section
- Your state's Department of Education
- The financial aid office at your college(s) of choice
- Your school guidance counselor

Your guidance counselor, in particular, can help you identify local scholarships and grants, including those offered by businesses, religious organizations, and civic groups who are looking for students just like you. If you have trouble getting started, try Taco Bell's Live Más Scholarship—they appreciate when you think outside the box (or bun, as they like to say).

Applications

While it may seem counterintuitive to start applying for scholarships before you've even picked out your university (or major), the earlier you start, the better. By starting early, you can take advantage of scholarships that are unique, creative, or cater to your extra-curricular activities and skills. It also gives you an opportunity to work out those pesky kinks in the application process. Here are some quick tips to help you once you reach the application phase in your scholarship hunt!

Manage Your Time

Whether you start applying for scholarships early or late in your high school career, the same rules apply, including learning time management. This season of life is a balancing act of schoolwork, sports, after-school programs, social life, college visits, and, of course, scholarship applications. By assigning a certain amount of time each week to scholarship searches and applications, you can determine how much time should be spent on each scholarship.

Collegiate True or False

Planning on having a part-time job while in college is a bad idea because the courses require so much study time.
[Answered at the end of the chapter.]

Just like any college or job application, doing it well requires attention to detail. Scholarship applications usually come with a list of requirements, so make sure every item on that list is checked. When it comes to scholarships, the best practice is to follow the guidelines exactly.

Once you've finished an application, set it aside for a day or two and then review it again with fresh eyes. Proofread and then proofread again, go over that checklist, and make sure everything looks clean and orderly. When everything is in place, make a copy for yourself in case something goes missing in transit.

Essays

Writing an essay isn't always a requirement when applying for scholarships. In fact, you will be able to apply for some scholarships simply by tweeting or posting videos to your social media accounts. As fun as flexing your social media game may be, knowing how to write a great essay is still an important asset in helping win a scholarship. While there are great books about writing college and scholarship essays, the following are some essential tips.

Stay on Topic

Every scholarship essay is slightly different—some will have a specific prompt while others will be open-ended and require a little creativity. Either way, sticking to the prompt will ensure you keep your paper on point. If the prompt is unclear to you or particularly challenging, underline the verbs and key words to help you identify the meaning of the assignment, or ask a writing teacher or parent if they understand it.

Once you have a clear understanding of the prompt, create an outline to organize your thoughts and get your ideas down. Use your organizational tools like Evernote or Google Docs to keep your outline—and your ideas—safe in the cloud.

Use Your Skills

Some scholarship essays will require you to be more personal than what you might be used to in your high school writing. Writing a research paper and writing a personal essay still use the same concepts of structure and form, so be sure to use clear, concise language and include the basic elements: an introduction (including your thesis), body paragraphs, and a conclusion.

Following the same procedure as with your application, set aside the essay for a day or two and then approach it from a fresh perspective. Spend time proofreading and have a family member or friend edit and proofread for you as well.

Check your grammar through a free tool, like *grammarly.com*. Just remember that sometimes the computer can't catch all the idiosyncrasies of the English language, and you should always be the final editor of your essay. Most importantly, be authentic in your essays—that's what scholarship committees are looking for.

Interviews

Many scholarships you apply for will not have an interview component, but for those that do, the process is similar to a job or college interview. Knowing your audience and appropriate preparation will help you feel ready for almost any question they might throw your way.

If the scholarship is related to sports, be prepared to answer questions about what you love about the game, what inspired you to start playing (and keep playing). For business-related scholarships, researching the company that is behind the scholarship and understanding their goal in offering it will provide insight into what made you stand out in your application. For leadership scholarships, prepare to answer questions about the leadership positions you held during your high school years.

Talk the Talk

Part of interviewing well is knowing how to be honest and authentic instead of simply trying to say the right things. Even if you are feeling under-qualified, focus on what you do well, your skills and passions, and why that makes you a good candidate for the scholarship. Also, speak positively and enthusiastically—it reminds the interviewers, and yourself, that you are excited about the prospect of the scholarship, going to college, and advancing your opportunities in life. Also, be yourself and stand out—chances are the interviewer will see lots of other applicants and you don't want to be lost in the mix.

Look the Part

Sometimes showing up to an interview dressed right is about more than looking professional. Cleaning up and grooming for the interview is certainly key, but keep in mind what the scholarship is for as you pick out your clothing. Is the scholarship creative in nature, focusing more on personality than academic merit? If so, don't be afraid to show a little personality with your choice of (professional) clothes. Whatever the scholarship, bear in mind that the interviewer is considering whether or not to hand you a sum of money, so showing up looking professional will speak volumes.

Starting early and knowing where and how to find scholarship opportunities can improve your chances of funding that college degree without debt, or at least with less financial burden to you and your family.

Now that you have the tools for finding the best and most beneficial scholarships, be sure to carry on your scholarship pursuit even after you enter your chosen college. As you pursue your degree, new scholarships and grants will become available, which means every year there are more options for paying down your tuition. There are scholarships waiting for you—your efforts will bring success!

My *Do College Right* Checklist

- o Start the scholarship hunt early in your junior year of high school.
- o Check in with your high school guidance counselor who will know about locally-sponsored scholarships. These often give you the best opportunity to win.
- o Have fun your senior year of high school, but stay focused on the time and effort required to obtain as much gift aid as possible for college.

Collegiate True or False

False. A part-time job is a great way to earn some spending money that might be in short supply after you pay for all your tuition, room and board, books, and fees. You will have adequate time to study, have a part-time job, enjoy activities and events, and hang out—IF you schedule your time well (more on this in Section 2).

During College

07

The Transition

THE WEEK NEW STUDENTS ARRIVE ON campus for orientation is one of my favorite weeks of every year. The energy level on campus is off the charts! It's been a long time since I had this starting-college experience myself, but I still remember feeling the butterflies of anticipation.

This is how one of our students described their first day:

> I vividly remember how it felt the morning my parents drove me over to Lakeland to begin my first year at Southeastern. Unsure of how to adjust, my stomach felt sick with

nerves. After all, I spent my entire life in the same town with the same familiar people. What would happen if I wasn't going to be comfortable away from my family? Also, how would I make new friends? Would college be too difficult? But within a matter of weeks, all of those doubts vanished thanks to the welcoming environment at SEU and some good advice I was given along the way.[17]

The transition into college life can be nerve-wracking. But you can take comfort in the fact that it is nerve-wracking for everyone. College is not just about attending classes; it's about jumping into life-changing opportunities that can help you grow intellectually, spiritually, and emotionally. The first few months of college offer plenty of opportunities to meet new people—you just have to put yourself out there.

Before I share some tips on how you can navigate the early weeks and months on campus, let me offer one idea that will help you more than any other: *self-discipline*. We all need more of this, and it's a personal quality that is developed throughout life. But all the advice in the world on "how to do college" won't benefit you too much if you don't hold yourself accountable and act responsibly. Ultimately, what success you find in college is up to you. The more you take responsibility for your life now, the better this experience will be. Plus, you will learn important lessons that will benefit you immensely after you don your gown and receive that diploma.

So, let's dive in! Needless to say, I won't try to cover every topic here—whole books are written about the transition into the college experience. But I do have some thoughts on how to help you get over the hump of challenges in the early weeks and months at school. You will have to study hard if you want to be successful in college, but that aspect will be much easier to deal with if you are having what I call "good fun" along the way. So, what's the secret sauce for enjoying college?

Planning and Scheduling

You will find college easier if you figure out a schedule for yourself and stick to it. You won't have mom or dad giving you any prompts, so eating, sleeping, classes, studying, social media, hanging out—all of those activities need some forethought and planning.

If you don't have one, I suggest getting a good weekly planner right away. Although you might be able to keep all of your important dates—deadlines, assignments, tests, appointments—on your phone or computer, I still think having a printed planner makes sense. After all, it won't run out of power at the worst possible moment! And just its presence in the backpack will remind you that there are meaningful things that need to get done.

Food, Sleep, Health

This is about as basic as it gets, but I'm surprised at how many students struggle with proper eating and rest. Too often these issues go together—too little rest may mean sleeping in and missing breakfast, which leads to poor concentration in class. It is also important to have some balance in your diet. You won't have anyone at school telling you to have some veggies with your burgers—you will have to make your own choices for balanced nutrition.

I know that inevitably there will be nights where you stay up late—perhaps even studying for the next day's test. But I urge you, as much as possible, go to bed and get a solid seven to eight hours of sleep each night. Life will go better the next day.

Get some exercise too. You may not be into sports or hanging out at the gym, but frequent, brisk walks around campus will do wonders for your physical and emotional well-being.

Collegiate True or False

*Because of their youthful energy and
strength, young adults can function well on six
hours of sleep per night.
[Answered at the end of the chapter.]*

Roommates

More than likely (unless you are a commuter stu-dent), you will begin college living in campus hous-ing. This means having one or more roommates. This new living arrangement will require some adjusting.

The best advice I have is to make a concerted effort early on to really get to know your room-mate(s). Find some commonality, which I realize may not come easy, but it's well worth it. One of your first meals should be with your roommate. Learn about each other's families, past, culture, and interests. Maybe work together to decorate your room and organize the furniture. Be open and share about your needs related to sleep, noise level, and visitors. Don't be passive aggressive—if something bothers you, graciously share it with your roommate.

Still, there will probably be some tensions,

such as, they:

- Go to bed earlier than you
- Get up earlier than you
- Don't shower enough
- Shower too long and there's no hot water
- Have their friends hang out in your room
- Are a neat freak
- Don't help keep the place clean
- Borrow your stuff without asking (on this one, don't hesitate to lock up valuables or even buy a small safe)

This list may make you want to buy a tent and live off campus, but there's a real positive side too—your roommate may become a friend for life. So, give this relationship your best shot.

As I've already said, a good first step to solving any tensions is to express yourself—calmly and kindly. Try to work it out. Keep in mind that you probably are doing things that annoy or freak out your roommate too. A good open conversation can do wonders for you both. But if you can't get over the hump in relating to your roommate, you may need some assistance from your residence assistant (RA).

You may want to live together all four years, or decide to go your separate ways after a semester or two. Either way, living closely with another

person is a valuable learning experience that is
hard to duplicate.

Friends

Making new friends may be the most important
part of successfully beginning your college life, so
it's well worth some intentional time and effort.
Most people, as they look back over the stages of
their life, agree that they met some of their best,
lifelong friends while in college. I'm sure there are
multiple reasons for this, but I think a maturing
self-understanding, combined with the freedom
to make more of your own choices, are the key
factors.

That's the positive outcome, but finding and
developing those new friendships can be challenging, particularly if you are more of an introvert.

Regardless, developing a few good friendships is
such a key part of "getting over the hump" as you
start college. Take some deep breaths, get ready to
leap, and abandon your comfort zone. In the first
two months of your freshman year, I suggest the
following:

- Make it a priority during your first semester
  to attend as many campus and dormitory
  events as possible and meet two new people
  each time. That includes concerts, sporting

events, intramurals, lectures, dorm floor parties—you get the picture.

- Join a club or organization. And volunteer to help—don't hang back!
- I know I'm repeating myself, but get to know your roommate/suitemate(s)—be intentional about asking to share some meals and attend events together.
- Introduce yourself to others on your floor or someone you meet in the lounge. This is not the time to be bashful. Remember—everyone is in the same boat during these early weeks and months.

Classes

Go to your classes! During your college career, there may be a few occasions where it makes some sense to skip a class. But don't make this a habit—you are paying a huge sum of money to learn from your professors. You will also meet people in class—some of them may become friends over time as you work on team projects and pursue the same major.

I also suggest making a personal connection with each of your professors within the first several weeks of each semester. I'm not talking about schmoozing or bringing them an apple, just appropriately introduce yourself after class. And if you have questions about the course's material, make an appointment to see the professor during their office hours. Your professors are there to give you knowledge and help you succeed.

Watch out for the alluring temptation of procrastination—it's a grade assassin. Gone are the days in high school when your teachers and parents would keep an eagle eye on your homework, projects, and upcoming tests. That's up to you now— build margin into your planning, work steadily, and give yourself adequate time to get things done. Avoid any caffeine-overloaded all-nighters by putting in the work all semester.

Activities

To be a college success, you will have to attend classes, study, and put in the time to flourish academically. That focus cannot be avoided. But, please, do not miss the opportunity to get involved in as many non-academic pursuits as your energy and schedule allow.

You may not be a varsity basketball player, but you can play on the dorm intramural team or play pickup basketball games at the gym. Did you play the trumpet in high school? How about joining a college pep band? Maybe you're interested in theater—they always need actors or backstage help. Maybe volunteering in the community to help elementary students improve their reading skills is your thing.

I know you will devote some time to playing video games, scrolling through social media, and hanging out with friends. But do yourself a huge favor—get out of your room, pack away the smartphone, go find some activities that are fun, and broaden your world.

Life Stewardship Tip #5

Welcome adventure and the unknown! If our lives were handed to us completely mapped out, there would be no discovery and no courage in making decisions and moving forward.

Looking Out for *You*

I close with this bit of advice: Your college experience is all about you. You are making a huge investment in your life—both now and way into the future. This is not the time to let friends or peers tell you what is best for you. You need to make your own choices, because you are now in the next life phase of further building your character and affirming your goals. Practically speaking this means:

• Growing in self-discipline

- Cultivating your spirituality and faith
- Eating and sleeping right
- Making peace with your roomie
- Having a few good friends—ones who help you grow and become a better person
- Going to class and keeping up with coursework
- Balancing study and play
- Not just passing courses, but becoming a lifelong learner

• • •

College is the launch pad into adult life. Though it can seem scary, you just have to take a leap of faith. I don't mean to oversimplify—this will be a difficult process. You are leaving home, perhaps for the first time, entering a new world, and meeting lots of new people. But remember the purpose of this transition—growth and self-discovery. College is one of the best times of your life to begin realizing your divine design.

My *Do College Right* Checklist

- o   What do you feel will be your biggest personal challenges in leaving home?
- o   What key things do you want to be sure to accomplish early in your freshman year?
- o   What are the activities at college you would really like to participate in?
- o   How can you take a step out of your comfort zone?

Collegiate True or False

False. The National Sleep Foundation recommends seven to nine hours of sleep per night for young adults, age 18-25, although in some cases six hours is adequate. Less than six hours is a definite "no-no."[32]

08

Faculty

WHEN CHOOSING YOUR COURSES, there's one important factor that students often overlook: *the faculty*. Your decisions related to your class schedule should not just be about *what you want to study*, but also *who you want to learn from*—who is best equipped to educate you.

What you want for certain from your education ROI is confidence that the knowledge you are receiving is of the highest quality, up to date, and relevant to the career path you are seeking. And it's not just the competence of the professors that is important; you also need to anticipate, as much as possible, how much personal attention you will receive from them. This last point is particularly important when you start taking courses in your chosen major.

Pracademic

A "pracademic" is not some type of dinosaur or potentially painful medical procedure! Pracademic is a more recently used term in higher education that combines the concepts of a person who is an academic but also a real-world practitioner in the related field. A pracademic professor is qualified to teach you the theory of your major, as well as offer valuable insight into how this theory actually works in the marketplace. Pracademics also may be more able to suggest meaningful internships, as well as help you find a job after you graduate—I'll discuss that in more depth later in this chapter.

As an example, at SEU we have an instructor in our political science department who once was a U.S. congressman. Not only are his courses enriched by his education and practical experience, but he also takes students on field trips to Washington, D.C., where he guides them through highly valuable learning opportunities because of the professor's relationships with government officials and staff.

It's probably not realistic nor necessary that all of your college instructors be pracademics, but it certainly would be good to have exposure to a few of them, so I recommend that you find out how many professors at your college have their feet in both worlds. You should be able to glean some of this information from the college's website or by asking your advisor.

Of course, the surer you can become of your major field, the better you will be prepared to evaluate each college's commitment to including successful pracademics on a particular department's faculty.

Faculty-Student Ratio

Often the student enrollment of a college or university is a good indicator of class sizes. At almost every college, regardless of student population, the class size of some general or very popular courses will be large—perhaps hundreds of students. That's not a huge issue, but you do want to determine how large the classes are in your major-specific courses.

The class sizes at private colleges are typically smaller than those at public state institutions. If class sizes are smaller, it will greatly heighten your opportunity to get to know the professor—and vice versa. You may have questions for the professor or be struggling with understanding certain concepts, and if the class size is smaller, you should be able to actually ask questions in class or talk to the professor after class concludes.

Perhaps even more critical than the faculty-student ratio is the issue of who is likely to teach most of your courses. I think it's only fair that the vast majority of your courses be taught by full professors or highly-qualified adjunct professors. Graduate students should generally only be used as the leaders in labs or other non-lecture settings. Often graduate students are very gifted in their chosen field, but they are still students.

Collegiate True or False

Although college professors are required to distribute a syllabus (summary and schedule) for each course, this is just a formality and most professors discard the syllabus during the semester. [Answered at the end of the chapter.]

Teaching vs. Research

Another issue to consider in evaluating faculty is the amount of research involvement by individual faculty members. This tends to be more of an issue at larger state or private institutions, and it has both positive and negative elements. If some professors are very active as researchers, this should mean they are more cutting edge in their fields—a benefit to their school and department. But it may mean they have less time to teach undergraduate

courses and/or be available to students. This is
something that you should be aware of, but probably will not be a deal maker or breaker in determining your course schedule.

Faculty Office Hours

Most students at some point in their college career hit a wall in a particular course. No matter
how much they study or seek help from other students, they still are not "getting it." If (or when)
this happens to you, please don't delay in visiting
the professor. Every professor has set office hours
when they are in their office and available to talk
with students. Normally this instructor will be glad
you came and offer the help you need. You may
feel uncomfortable going to meet your professor
during office hours, but remember that this is part
of what you are paying the university for.

Know Your Professors

Getting to know your professors enriches your education experience; it is also helpful later on down
the road when you need a recommendation from a
professor for a job or scholarship. If you are more
of an introvert, this task may require a courage
boost! You can do it—breathe deeply and go introduce yourself to the professor after class and ask a

question about the material. You could also meet your professor during office hours if that is less intimidating to you. If you are more of an extrovert, stepping out and connecting with the professor may not be as hard. Regardless of your personality, *make yourself known*.

I'm not talking here, of course, of any kind of schmoozing or the like. Don't be "that guy" or "that girl" who always asks a question in class that turns into a monologue. Use common sense in your connections with teachers. But be sure they know your name! Again, this will be easier to accomplish if the faculty-student ratio is lower. With fewer students in the class, the faculty member will be better able to observe and evaluate as you speak, write, and participate. The professor may even provide more insight into your gifts and abilities than you were aware of before. As I've mentioned earlier, this is exactly what happened to me in my first year of college as two different professors recognized my skill sets. Most professors have been doing this for many years and with hundreds or even thousands of students—just like you.

Look for opportunities outside of the classroom to meet and become acquainted with professors, particularly those in your major. One of the things I benefited from personally was personal connections I made with faculty members outside of classes. Some professors will be advisors or sponsors to

college clubs and organizations, so if you participate in these you may be able to connect in a more
relaxed, social environment. Do not neglect even
the simple act of just asking to meet with a professor who may not be in your major's department or
even at your school.

Faculty Help with Internships and Jobs

If some of your professors are also involved in a
profession or other position in the world outside
the campus, they will have contacts and networking resources that help land internships and jobs.
As I will state so emphatically in chapter 12, your
involvement in internships throughout your four
years can make all the difference in landing a
great job after graduation. Internships are surefire
resume builders, which your professors can often
help with.

In our business department at SEU, we have
pracademics who are also employed by local companies, such as Lockheed Martin. These companies sponsor internships, and a number of our
graduates have ended up with full-time jobs with
these employers after they interned. Many of our
school of education graduates have a similar experience—moving from student teaching spots to
full-time teaching positions upon graduation.

• • •

In conclusion, I urge you to be intentional in maximizing opportunities to connect with college faculty—in the classroom and outside the classroom. This is another part of your life stewardship—making the most of integrating your passions with the ways you can acquire the knowledge and experience that ultimately will land you in a career that rewards you professionally and financially.

My *Do College Right* Checklist

○ How easy—or hard—do you think it will be for you to make contact with your college professors? How might you overcome any anxiety about meeting with a professor?

○ If your parents attended college, ask them what they liked or disliked about their professors? What advice can they give you?

Collegiate True or False

False. You should treat the syllabus like the "bible" for the course and put important deadlines in your personal planner. If a professor makes a change in the syllabus (hopefully not on a day you skip class!), then adjust your planner accordingly.

09

The Classroom

Grades are not the most important thing. I know—shocking. What I mean by this "shocking" statement is that the college experience should be about many important things and, certainly, grades are on the list. But grades are not as important as *learning*. It would be a very disappointing outcome—after you have made a sizable investment of time and money—for you to finish college feeling like you didn't learn that much. Having a great grade point average does not always directly translate to how much you learned. My favorite way I like to express my point on this topic is: *education is not a place you go; education is your life.*

In today's fast-paced, ever-changing world, your ability to learn will most likely take you further in a chosen career than how high your grade point average was in college. A commitment to lifelong learning is what will allow you to bring your best self to the context and challenges of whatever job or situation you are in. Having said that, I will say that what happens in the classroom is very important. This is where you will intersect with teachers who, based on their expertise and experience, can show you the information that is necessary to learn and retain.

Of course, to meet degree requirements and complete college successfully, you should pay careful attention to your grade point average. For example, your ability to retain scholarships as an undergraduate or even receive new ones will be dependent on a solid GPA. My hunch is that the more you develop the qualities of a good learner, the higher your grade point average will be. And when it comes time for job interviews when you finish college, potential employers will sense that you are not just skilled at getting good grades, but that you are a mature person who can be trusted to learn on the job. So now that I've made my plea for you to strive to be a lifelong learner, let me share some tips on getting good grades.

The ABCs of Good Grades

This may surprise you—your GPA has less to do

with your intelligence level and more to do with your self-discipline. This is why I can guarantee you that if you follow my grade ABCs, you will get good grades, become a better learner, and finish college successfully.

A–Always Turn Something In

I've observed most students' academic problems begin because they simply don't turn in their work. There are plenty of reasons students don't turn in their work on time: busyness, laziness, or poor time management. Even really responsible students may not turn an assignment in because they feel unable to complete it *perfectly*. But turning in *something* is always better than turning in nothing—even if it's not complete or exactly how you want it. No matter what the challenging issues or reasons are, just turn in your work! Remember that planner I told you to get? Write down when all your assignments are due in your planner and map out how much time you think you'll need to complete an assignment. Schedule in time to work on it throughout the week before it's due; this way you won't be surprised when the due date comes.

What you need to remind yourself is that your professors are not looking for ways to trip you up or fail you. In fact, it's just the opposite: they want you to *learn* and succeed. But you have to complete your side of the agreement: come to class, study the material, and **A**lways turn in your assignments.

Life Stewardship Tip #6

Preparation is the glue that will keep you grounded through the chaos of change.

B–Be in Class

You can't know what your professor wants you to learn and retain—and reflect in assignments and tests— if you aren't in class!

Again, I'm always amazed by the looks of abject panic I see on the faces of some students during the last days of the semester. Many of them look quite worn out—probably because they're exhausted after pulling all-nighter study binges. Part of their dilemma is that in order to pull their final grade from the abyss, they need an A+ on the final. Mournfully they murmur, "I didn't know this [hugely important] assignment was due!" The professor probably announced the assignment five times during the semester, but the students weren't in class to hear about it. Being in class not only guarantees that you will learn more about the subject, but also that you won't miss important deadlines.

When you go to class, don't slink in and slump

in the back row of the classroom. Participate in class—make yourself known to the professor and your classmates. Getting to know your classmates is a great way to find people you can study with, and hopefully will help you understand the material better. So, do yourself and your grade point a huge favor: **B**e in class.

C–Call Your Professor

College is an exciting time where you will experience many new things. As you grow to be an independent adult, you will experience freedom, but you will also be faced with many challenges and setbacks. College will challenge you in areas you have never been challenged in before. You are going to find some areas of deficiency, skills you haven't quite fully grasped yet, and that's okay! If we are going to be lifelong learners, that means we have a lot to learn. If we are going to be teachable, that means we have to accept that we have holes in our knowledge.

In college, as everywhere else, life is going to happen—unexpected events out of your control will influence and affect you. In both cases—deficient skills or unforeseen events—your professors are your best resource. They don't want you to fail their class or feel like you need to prioritize school before everything in your life (most professors at least). If they know what is happening in your life, often they can get you helpful resources no matter what your situation is. So, don't be timid about asking for help; when appropriate, give your professor a **C**all.

Collegiate True or False

Some college professors grade on a curve;
other professors do not.
[Answered at the end of the chapter.]

The Rest of the Alphabet

Now that you have my ABCs for good grades, here are a few other ideas that will complete your alphabet on how to keep on top of your academics.

Take Responsibility

This isn't high school anymore and mom or dad won't be telling you to do your homework. It's up to you to stay on top of your responsibilities. Make plans and keep them—weekly planning is best. Remember that advice to buy a good planner? Incorporate your class requirements in that planner. This will help you manage your time well. I've observed that a lot of failure in college is a result of poor time management.

Seek Advice

Learn from anyone and everyone you can—professors, advisors, and fellow students. Listen to your advisor and take the courses you need to complete your degree program on time. Talk to other students about how they manage their time. Get to know others in your classes—maybe even setting times to study together and ask their advice on things you are struggling with. This can be a good way to improve your understanding of the course material and make new friends in the process. Most colleges offer numerous services to help you improve your skills and grades. For example, if you are weaker in essay writing, check out the writing lab. It's not a sign of weakness to seek help—in fact, it's a strength!

Know Your Limits

Don't sign up for twenty hours of coursework in a semester. Remember, academics should be part of your college experience, not the whole ballgame. Make sure you aren't spending all your time studying. Set healthy boundaries for yourself and make sure you are thriving in every area of your life.

Take Notes

Take notes in class. You might do this on your computer or you might even go old school with a pen and notebook. It doesn't matter what format you take notes on as long as you're taking notes. When you make a note, your brain gets the message that *this is something to be remembered.* This will be valuable during a quiz, studying for tests, and taking the final. You can also record the lecture on your phone if you learn better that way, just make sure to get your professor's permission first.

Learn How You Best Study

If you buckle down and study on a daily basis, you should have plenty of time for all the fun things you want to do in college. If you have a proclivity for procrastination, find people to study with who will hold you accountable. It might also be helpful for you to have a specific place to study— your own study cave, one might say. You have to find some place where you can do concentrated studying. How you best concentrate is your unique preference, but find the spot and go there on a regular—daily—basis. And, I suggest turning off your phone and social media when you are holed up in the cave. I also recommend studying six days a week and not studying at all one day of the week. Do restful, fun things on that day and recharge. If God needed a day to rest when creating, maybe you do too. Studying is hard work, so it is necessary to reward yourself. Did you put in a hard three hours of productive studying in your cave? Sounds like it's time for a coffee, ice cream, or an episode of your favorite show!

· · ·

I really believe that if you follow these ABCs and other advice, your grades will be fine and college will become one of the greatest experiences of your life. And remember: *grades aren't the most important thing!*

My *Do College Right* Checklist

o How do you respond to the statement, "grades aren't the most important thing"? Agree or disagree? How do you plan to balance academics and other activities in college?

o What study routines have worked well for you in the past? How might you duplicate that in the new college environment?

Collegiate True or False

True. Often a professor will describe his or her grading approach in the course syllabus or explain it during the first class session. They might explain a specific grading approach on a particular assignment or test—more reasons to always Be in class!

010

Changing
Majors

IF YOU ARE LIKE MANY STUDENTS, AT some point in your college years you will think about changing your major. So, don't be alarmed if you seem to lose your passion for the career path you once were so certain of. Changing majors carries the notion that "if you really have your act together, you really will just *know* when you start college what you want to do with your life." The truth? Life is not that simple; what's more important is gaining clarity of your divine design and making needed adjustments to maximize the blending of your passion and gifts to find a satisfying career.

According to research, **almost a third of first-time college students change their**

major at least once within three years, and about one in ten students change majors twice.[18]

Being undecided for the first year or two may in fact be a good path—as long as you are sincerely looking for your major. Having an undeclared major allows you to take core classes so that once you decide your major, you will be able to load your schedule with major-specific courses. While undeclared, it is helpful to figure out if you lean more toward liberal arts, business, or STEM (science, technology, engineering, math), as some of the core classes will have different options depending on which track you're on.

Although this entire book is designed to help you make the most of your higher education, perhaps the most helpful thing I can communicate is, during these years of your life, feel free to experiment and find out what it is you *really want to do*. And that may involve changing your college major.

Collegiate True or False

You will lose many of your course credits if you change majors in your junior year.
[Answered at the end of the chapter.]

To Change or
Not to Change?

I've seen some students switch majors once—or more—and they end up getting quite frustrated with their college experience and decide to drop out. Finishing college is a big deal that no one can ever take away. Graduating may, in the long run, be more important than your specific major or degree. One study found that only about 27 percent of undergraduate degree holders were working in a job directly related to their college major.[19]

As you consider changing majors, be sure you understand as clearly as possible why you are having second thoughts now about your major. Is this a recent development or have you been wondering about your major for some time? Be sure you know that you are not being motivated by circumstances—a bad grade in a class or relationship problems might make you feel like you need to change the course you're on. Dig deep and let your goals speak louder than your current feelings and circumstances. Process your possible change with others who can help you see all sides of such a significant adjustment. Your academic advisor, your parents, a mentor, the career placement department at your school, a pastor or spiritual guide—all of them want to assist as you consider this option.

Having said all that, if you believe changing

your major is the right thing to do, particularly if you are in your first or second year, you certainly can do this—thousands of college students do it every year! And it's far better to make a change now than to continue in your current major, graduate, get a job, and then find out five years down the road that you really dislike what you're doing.

I have a few more issues I want you to consider concerning a major change:

- What will this cost you in time and money?
- If you change majors, are you still at the right school or might it be necessary to transfer?
- Evaluate other potential losses. If changing your major means transferring to another school, you will have to start over again in all aspects of college life—not just academics, but very important things like friendships, housing, organizations, part-time work, and more.
- Have you done an internship related to your new major and intended career that is adding insight on this decision? Internships can either confirm your college major or call it into question.
- Again, if you are in your first year or two— let's say under about sixty credit hours, then a change may not be catastrophic because

you have not taken that many upper-level courses. If you are in your junior year, proceed with more care. Generally speaking, if you still plan to graduate in four years, you should not change your major after you start your junior year.

- Consider all possible options: How about a double major? Maybe change your minor but keep your major? Make your major your minor? A second degree? Keep your major but settle on pursuing a graduate degree that better matches your ultimate career goals? An academic advisor can help you see all possibilities before you decide what to do.

- If you are planning to go to graduate school, perhaps your current major won't affect that path significantly. In other words, sticking with your major may be the best short-term choice to reduce the time spent on and cost of your bachelor's degree.

Life Stewardship Tip #7

Life may deal you lemons, but that doesn't mean you have to live as though you were biting into one. Joy, just like misery, is a matter of choice and attitude.

Something to keep in mind: as I've mentioned, many students graduate with a particular major but within a few years find themselves in a job or even a career that was unanticipated. Who you are as a person—your character, experience, skills and interests, flexibility, and job reviews—becomes more important than your major over time. This being the case, finishing college on time and within your budget may be more beneficial than having a specific major in the long run.

A Plan for Changing Your Major

You've decided to make a change. Here are some steps to follow to make this process as easy as possible for you.

1. Review your design and passions. I've already mentioned this but don't skip this opportunity for some self-assessment of who you are, your skills, and your dreams.
2. Go see your faculty advisor. Hopefully you have some relationship with your advisor and can speak honestly about your concerns. If you think your advisor is too committed to keeping you in your current major, go to your school's career placement department and speak to a general studies

advisor. If you are considering a transfer, an advisor at another school may also provide helpful information to guide your decision.

3. Be sure you will qualify for your new major. If you are switching departments within your college or university, talk to an advisor within the major you want to transfer into about GPA requirements and other factors

4. Do the work. Be sure to check out the job outlook in the new field you are considering. Research all the possible career paths and try to schedule some informational interviews with people in those fields.

5. Consult with your parents. They probably have a large stake in your education—good communication with them is a must.

6. Determine how to maximize the course credits you already have. Sometimes transferring to a different school is necessary depending on the major you choose. If a transfer seems necessary, very carefully determine how many of your hours will be accepted by the new school. There is a website devoted to transfers that may provide assistance: *www.collegetransfer.net.*

7. Make the switch official by completing all necessary applications and paperwork.

• • •

I have one last piece of information to share that may encourage you: Research has found that **students who change majors actually graduate at a higher rate than those who don't**.[20] I think that may be because a thoughtful change in your major probably means an adjustment that puts you on a more focused path to finding the career that is best suited for you.

My *Do College Right* Checklist

o   In your own words, describe why you might want to change your major.

o   What are five potential jobs available for the major you are planning to pursue?

Collegiate True or False

False. Whether or not you lose credits depends more on what major (or different college) you switch to—not the year you make the change. However, changing in your junior year means you may have already taken upper-level courses that will not apply to upper-level course requirements for another major.

011

Extracurricular Activities

WE'VE LEARNED THAT GRADES AREN'T the most important thing. Now I want to say something that may be equally as crucial if you are going to get the most out of your college experience: have as much "good fun" as possible! I have observed thousands of college students, and the ones who graduate after four years and seem best prepared for the next step are the ones who learned a lot *and* had tons of fun.

So, what kind of fun am I proposing? *Good fun.* I'm not advocating for what many people may think is "fun"—experimenting with alcohol or drugs, partying, and the like. Those things actually can be fun killers and may destroy the opportunity to have an awesome college experience.

By good fun, I mean exploring new interests, meeting and making new friends, enjoying the many activities and campus events your school provides, participating in intramural sports, joining campus clubs and organizations, and maybe even running for a student government position. All of these experiences will help you better understand your divine design and contribute to you becoming a well-rounded, mature person—spiritually, emotionally, intellectually, socially, and even physically.

My advice in a nutshell to an undergraduate student: study hard, learn hard, play hard. A great college experience is holistic—both in and out of the classroom. Get involved in clubs, social events, and dorm experiences. By being active, particularly in activities that you really enjoy, you will get to know people who share your interests. Friendships will form, and some of them will turn into relationships that may last a lifetime.

Since I have always enjoyed involvement in leadership, when I was in college one of my fun activities was student government. This turned out to be a fantastic choice for several reasons. At Vanguard University, I was twice elected vice president of the student body. I really liked student government because it gave me an opportunity to work on my leadership skills and live out my life mission of helping others. I experienced the added benefit of making friends in the organization, and I am still friends with some of them to this day. In fact, during one of those years, I met a young woman I really liked. In fact, I liked her so much that later I married her! We're now in our third decade of marriage, so I'm really glad I didn't study all the time while in college.

Get Involved

When you arrive on campus, don't wait to get involved in extracurricular activities. Even before you arrive for your freshman orientation, you can begin thinking about the extracurricular opportunities available on campus by checking out the school's website. You might be able to start following organizations on social media.

When you arrive on campus, within a week or so there will be some type of activities fair where all of the groups on campus will have information tables for the purpose of recruiting new members. Be bold—those upperclassmen on the other side of the table were just like you a year or so ago! Ask questions and get the details on potential clubs and organizations. Go ahead and sign up for information from all that stir your interest. It may take weeks or even months to find the right balance of time and energy you can commit to extracurricular activities, but at the beginning, keep your interests broad. Later on, you will better understand what most excites you and how much time you can commit.

Don't just gravitate to the types of clubs you joined in high school—branch out, try new things. There are many activities that your high school might not have even offered, and you won't know if you like it until you try it. For example, you might have a knack for water skiing, but you won't know unless you join the recreational water skiing club. You may not plan to be a theater major, but you can help out with campus productions. Maybe you've always been interested in photography, so join the photography club. Now is your chance to learn more about your interests with people who are interested in the same things.

Joining organizations associated with your major is a great way to learn more about your future profession, network with people in the same field, build your resume, and be aware of the opportunities available to you as a student. If you are a business major, you might want to join the American Marketing Association. If you're an education major, you might want to join the Student Education Association. I encourage you to talk to your advisor about the organizations associated with your major.

An extracurricular activity you may not have included on your list is a job on campus. Having a job on campus will not only give you some extra spending money but will also expose you to staff members and other students—who knows, this experience may prompt an interest that even leads to a career choice.

Remember that students who are involved in at least one campus organization will show greater college satisfaction and are more likely to graduate.[21] Explore the opportunities available to you, try out a few organizations, and find some that work with your schedule and interests. Research confirms that "feeling you belong" has a significant influence not only on how enjoyable your college experience will be, but even may be the reason you stick it out and graduate.[22]

Life Stewardship Tip #8

Every experience—good and bad—is part of how you are shaped, molded, and crafted into a force of change in the world. God is not just a great Creator, He's a master Recycler!

An Incomprehensive List of Activities

I won't even try to list all the extracurricular options on a college campus as each school will have some unique options. Here is a list, though, of some types of extracurricular activities to get you thinking about what might interest you during your college years:

- Academic (honor societies)
- Arts (music, theater)
- Athletic (intramural sports)
- Campus-wide Events (homecoming, parents' weekend, orientation)
- Media (newspaper, yearbook, radio/TV)
- Greek (fraternities and sororities)
- Multi-cultural
- Political (college Democrats, Republicans, Independents, Libertarians)
- Religious
- Student Government
- Volunteer and Service

There are numerous organizations in each one of these categories, so you are guaranteed to find one you like. And if you arrive on campus and have an interest you are passionate about but there is no club in existence, you can start an organization yourself—it's easier than it sounds!

Collegiate True or False

Almost all long-term friendships made while in college start with a social media contact.
[Answered at the end of the chapter.]

How Good Fun Leads to a Good Career

Extracurricular activities have a great value in and of themselves—good fun needs no particular justification! However, there is another benefit you may not have thought of: just as your high school extracurricular activities counted a great deal in your acceptance to the college of your choice, so too your extracurricular activity involvement in college may pave the way to a job after you graduate.

Potential employers want to find bright students who are also good learners, adept communicators, and cooperative team players. Your involvement with an organization will communicate to an employer that you have a good work ethic and desirable character. They will see that you value activities and associations. It will also demonstrate that you can manage your time well.

Who knew that your volunteer work with students at a nearby middle school, for example, would be the difference-maker in convincing a re-cruiter with a major corporation that you would be a great fit for the open position at their company? Having good fun in college will greatly benefit you during college, as well as long after you graduate.

My *Do College Right* Checklist

- o What is one interest or activity you have always wanted to pursue but haven't yet?
- o Ask your advisor about or research organizations specific to your major. Try to find a good work/play balance. Say you have fifty hours a week, how many hours do you need for going to class and studying and how many for good fun?

Collegiate True or False

False. Actually, I don't have quantitative research to prove my answer, but I think social media may help you connect with others on campus. I believe in-person interactions in a variety of academic and extra-curricular settings will better yield the rich friendships that may last a lifetime.

012

Internships

INTERNSHIPS ARE THE PERFECT opportunities to figure out exactly what you want to do. You are able to get an inside look at future careers and evaluate whether or not the job or company is a good fit for you. I am a huge fan of college internships because my own career was jump-started by an internship I had while in community college. As I mentioned before, when I left high school, I was not precisely sure what career field to pursue, but I knew I wanted to do something within the field of communications. I was able to intern at a local TV station, and eventually that internship turned into a full-time job as a sports broadcaster. I realize that my story is unusual in how rapidly an internship can lead to a real job, but the takeaway from my experience is this: *internships build your resume and often are difference-makers in receiving job offers.*

Today, many employers will not even look at college graduates who have not had an internship or other practical job experience.[23] Research has found that of the college graduates who completed a paid internship, 63 percent received a job offer, compared to 35 percent who never interned. Also, **graduates with paid internships received a starting salary that was 28 percent higher than their peers without internship experience**.[24] I have observed this at SEU as well; the students who have the easiest time finding a job are those who had multiple internships, were active in extracurricular activities, and had some leadership experience in a campus organization or in student government. Obviously, internships can lead to more and better job offers after college, but there are other benefits too.

Collegiate True or False

An internship even after you graduate from college may prove valuable.
[Answered at the end of the chapter.]

I encourage our students at Southeastern University to start seeking internship opportunities as soon as they get settled on campus. Here's why:

- **Industry, Professional, or Career Knowledge** – An internship might confirm your desire to pursue a particular major and career—or convince you that you need to pursue other options. Internships help you discover what kind of job you actually enjoy doing. Either way, the experience contributes to your ultimate success.

- **Course Credit** – Some colleges offer course credit for completed internships. Check if your school offers this opportunity.

- **Networking** – While working at your internship, you will interact with supervisors and co-workers who might become the source of a future job or perhaps agree to write a letter of recommendation when your post-college job search begins. Maybe someone you meet will also agree to be a mentor while you are still in college or even later when you begin your career. In other words, be professional and really nice to the people you meet at your internship!

- **Resume Builder** – A list of internships

may be the highlight of your resume to potential employers. Let's face it, you will be competing with thousands of students who may be able to meet or surpass your GPA or list of extracurricular achievements, but they may not be able to compete with the practical experience you gained via internships.

- **Your First "Real Job" Opening** – One research study showed that 53 percent of employed graduates received their job from an employer or organization where they had interned while a student.[25] At SEU, for example, over 90 percent of our students in Education get jobs before they graduate. The business where you do your internship may be hiring when you graduate. You may be first in line for that job opening since they already know you and have seen what you can do.

- **Self-Confidence Enhancement** – You will feel better about your professional abilities after an internship where you learned new skills, met new people, and accomplished new tasks. All of these achievements will set you up for success in your college courses, as well as confidence when you begin interviewing for a job.

What's more valuable than having the right answers is learning how to ask the right questions.

Ingle Internship Plan

By now you probably are aware that I like to help others by suggesting plans that lead to success. So, I have a plan for securing internships. Here are the steps:

- **Think first about your divine design and passions** – This is always important as you make decisions—start here, too, when considering the type of internship you should seek. If you are interested in a career in the marketing of women's shoes, then you should look for an internship with a company that manufactures or distributes women's shoes. If you want to be a high school athletic trainer, find out if any local fitness clubs have an opportunity to assist one of their trainers.

- **Investigate internship opportunities in your department** – Your professors may know of internships that would be great for you—even some that are already approved for credit. At SEU, for example, several of the professors work at local corporations.

- **College career placement center** – In your first year, you should become acquainted with the career center at your university. This place will help you in multiple ways while you're a student: you can find assistance in preparing your resume, writing cover letters, interview practice, and finding internships.

- **Connections** – Many students receive internships via family connections. Who in your family—immediate and beyond—works for an employer that might have an internship of interest to you? What businesses in your hometown might have an internship opportunity?

- **Internet** – *Internships.com* advertises the availability of over 75,000 internships. The database is searchable by keyword and location. *Indeed.com* is touted as the most powerful job and internship listing service on the web. Use the advanced search function and select internships from the "show jobs by type" tab.

Paid or Unpaid?

Naturally, if you can find an internship that is a good fit for you and offers a paycheck, that's wonderful! The good news is that many employers do pay their interns—71 percent in a recent study.[26] But maybe even more important than the money is the type of experience you will receive—specifically, does it match well with your intended career?

If you must earn money during the summer to stay in school, then certainly keep seeking a paid internship. If the financial aspect is not quite as important, then the impact of an unpaid internship on your future resume may be worth the loss of money.

Increasingly, a solid internship in the career field you are planning on pursuing after college is a great way to stretch your abilities, gain experience, and acquire real world job skills. Potential employers will definitely take notice. Sometimes taking an unpaid internship is necessary in order to get the experience you need for your future career. I urge you to do as many internships as possible during your undergraduate years.

My *Do College Right* Checklist

- o If you could have your pick, what would be your dream internship?
- o Is there any reason you cannot pursue that dream internship?
- o What's your Plan B if the dream internship doesn't happen?

Collegiate True or False

True. If you have not yet found the job you really want after graduation, another internship in your chosen industry—or even with a favorite company—may be the path to an entry-level position.

Graduation and Beyond

013

Job Search

AFTER ALL THE HARD WORK, LATE-night study sessions, getting up early for class—not to mention all the fun—the time has come for the next stage of the journey: getting a job. Your passions and gifts led you to choose a college where you felt you could both learn and flourish as a person. And, hopefully, a part of your college decision was finding a school with a good record of their graduates finding quality jobs in their career fields.

When looking for a job, your attitude may be the most important factor. This is a situation in life when being an outside-the-box thinker is advantageous. Be alert at all times to clues that may lead to a job. Be disciplined in looking for work! Now that your college career is coming to a close, your primary "job" in the coming months is to find a job. Finding a job is usually hard work; prepare yourself for some long hours and days of researching and filling out applications. The faculty, staff, and career placement office at your college will help in any way possible, but no one—including your university—will be able to hand you a job when you graduate. Your college years have given you the opportunity to understand better who you are and how you can use your gifts and skills to make a contribution in this world.

Your undergraduate degree has helped you become a critical thinker so that you can analyze, discern, and understand what's the right thing for you to do as a satisfying career. The next step is up to you. I wish I could promise that after gaining your degree employers will be lining up to offer you the job of your dreams. Just be thankful you have the degree because this greatly improves your chances of employment. According to the Bureau of Labor Statistics, the unemployment rate for those with a bachelor's degree or higher was at 2.1 percent as of April 2018.[27] While that is a significant difference from the 3.9 percent unemployment rate of those with a only a high school diploma, just because the likelihood of employment is higher for college graduates doesn't mean a job is guaranteed.

The key to finding the right job, frankly at any time in your career, is to stay self-aware and self-disciplined. When you understand clearly who you are, your gifts, and what you are about, then you will look for the right kind of opportunities and will make good decisions when job prospects come along. My own job trajectory, starting way back in community college, was accelerated due to my self-awareness and self-discipline. Because I knew what my general interests were, I was able to recognize opportunities when they came. At every stage of my career, when a new door has opened, I've been able to sense almost immediately whether I should say yes or no to any new job opportunity because of the self-awareness I have cultivated over the years.

Evaluate Jobs and Employers

While you may be very eager to start your career right after graduation, it is important to remember to evaluate employers and job opportunities to make sure you find a good fit. This will ensure that you begin to build your career and will prevent you from burning out quickly. As you encounter potential jobs, ask yourself some questions:

- Will this job allow me to display my talents?
- What are the tasks and expectations—do they align with my talents, education, skill

set, and experience?

- What does the employer want to accomplish through this position?
- Do the company's values align with my values?

Research

Research potential career paths and jobs. Although you may have graduated with a specific major and career path in mind, it may not be clear how to apply what you've learned to the job market. Begin by researching which jobs are available and narrow in on the ones that match your skill set and interests. Today's labor market is in constant flux, so in your career you may find many ways to use your skills. Your skills may be a great match for a job in an industry you have not considered. Become adept in searching and invest significant time in mining the Internet for job opportunities.

Make Use of College Career Placement Services

As I've suggested earlier in this book, it's wise to start connecting with the placement office at your college even as early as your freshman year. This department in most colleges will connect you to internship opportunities, assist with resume preparation, hold mock job interviews, and have job listings. The dean's office of your college major may also provide networking opportunities and job listings in your career field. And if some of your professors are involved in pracademic endeavors, they may be aware of openings.

List Employers You Would Like to Work For

This is the time to dream! Who would you like to work with? Start with employers in the area, region, and state where your college is located—then go national, maybe even international. Learn as much as you can about each company and create a file for future reference. Start following them on social media. When the opportunity arises, make direct contact.

Write Your Resume

Although the resume may not carry quite the weight it once did, with networking being a more important factor, you still need a great resume that presents you and your qualifications creatively and strategically for today's marketplace. It is important to remember that employers are looking for a well-rounded candidate—someone who was a good student with a good GPA (not necessarily a perfect GPA). They will also look to see if you were active in clubs and campus events. Employers will look to see if you held any leadership positions in student government or in organizations you were a part of. Put all of this information on your resume to show you are a well-rounded candidate. I have observed that the students who have the easiest time finding jobs are those who had a nice balance between academics and activities while on campus.

I urge you to get resume-building advice from your college career office, or from anyone who has extensive resume experience. There are various computer software programs now that are used to mechanically search resumes for key words that match job descriptions. It is important to carefully target your resume and cover letter for every job you apply for, because if your resume doesn't contain a certain amount of the key words, it might not even be looked at! Make sure to use the language used in the job description on your resume and cover letter.

If you've sent your resume and haven't heard back from the company, after about seven days you can follow up with them. This shows initiative, and it will help you know if you need to look for other opportunities.

Build a Personal Website and Blog

Another way to market yourself is to build a personal website or blog. You may feel like you don't have too much to offer yet related to your career field, but you can creatively reveal how you are preparing to be a productive contributor in the future. This is also a good opportunity to display or provide a link to your resume.

Review Your Social Media Profiles

Hopefully you have not been "wild and crazy" on social media. This is the time to start looking at your public social media "face" as though you are a recruiter for a major corporation. And in addition to deleting anything that may give the wrong impression, start enhancing your profile with information that highlights your personal qualities, interests, and volunteer activities. Just be honest, real, and strategic.

Contact References

Soon you will need to supply references to interested employers. Don't wait until the last minute. Ask several references if they would be willing to be listed as references on job applications.

Network

Talk to everybody and anybody. Even start with family and friends—you may have a little-known relative who knows of a job. Be very aware of the "hidden job market." It's been found that as high as 85 percent of jobs are filled via networking.[28] Usually these jobs are filled through a wide variety of informal, personal contacts.

Create a LinkedIn Profile

LinkedIn is a great way to look for jobs and to market yourself to potential employers. Keep updating the profile with information on your activities, college coursework, awards, etc. This will be one of your best opportunities to connect with and make yourself known to professionals in your career field. Make as many contacts as possible—particularly with alumni from your college.

We are in the social media age where you have to find ways to be seen and discovered. More than likely, a potential employer will not come knock on the door of your room or apartment. So, use your computer and communicate often and in varying ways. And when you network or send messages to potential employers, always type your messages in a word processor first to make sure your writing is clear and free of errors. When you have it right, then paste it into an email or other message.

> ## Collegiate True or False
>
> *Social media should not be*
> *used to find a job.*
> *[Answered at the end of the chapter.]*

Tap into Your College's Alumni Network

Connect with recent graduates who can offer advice on job hunting in today's marketplace. The alumni from your school may really want to help you find work, because they were in your shoes awhile back. There should be a database on campus that will give you names of alums in your career field. Meet as many alumni as possible when they are on campus for homecoming or other alumni-oriented events.

Meet Recruiters

Keep a sharp eye out for employers visiting campus to interview job candidates. Keep in mind that your skill set may match an employer's wish list even though your major may not seem a perfect fit for a particular company. Think out of the box and present yourself creatively.

Job Fairs

Are you interested in a particular type of industry that holds seminars you might attend? How about going as a student participant? Career events are great places to learn and network. Attend any in your locale. Don't be bashful—talk to any recruiters who will listen. Have resumes with you to hand out.

Interviews

You will find plenty of information online about job interviews. Also, your career placement office will have information and may even provide a mock interview opportunity. Practice, practice, practice—even with your peers. Interviews are hard to come by in our competitive job market—particularly since there is so much dependence on online sharing of candidate information. Remember that job interviews are just as much about you interviewing the potential employer as they are about them interviewing you. Use the interview time to make sure that the job you are applying for would be a good fit for you.

Set Yourself Apart

When the opportunity comes for an interview, be ready and arrive early! Right after the interview, if you're so inclined, you can write a handwritten note or email thanking the interviewer for their

time and for considering you for the position. This
is one simple thing you can do to set yourself apart
from other applicants.

Informational Interviews

This is both an opportunity to learn more about
your intended career as well as meet the people
who might have job openings—now or in the future. So, contact some companies you are interested in and ask for the opportunity to have an informational interview about the work they do. This
is not a job interview—you are sincerely going to
a business to learn more about their type of work.
Prepare, though, like it is a job interview—dress
right, have copies of your resume with you, etc.
But don't ask for a job!

Prepare Your Elevator Pitch

If you are talking with someone, whether in an interview or not, and he or she asks you, "Tell me
what kind of career and job you are looking for—
why are you qualified?" will you be ready to give
a compelling answer in thirty seconds? To prepare
for this—write out your answer, polish it, then
memorize it so you could say it in your sleep. You
never know when you are going to need to "sell
yourself" in an instant.

Other Options

Sometimes, full-time job opportunities aren't available right away. It can be frustrating to spend weeks or longer looking for a job and not coming across anything that works for you. I want to let you know that there are other options you can consider as you wait for the perfect full-time job opportunity to come your way.

Part-time Job

If you are still looking for the great full-time position, consider finding a part-time position with companies of interest to you. A large percentage of job openings are never publicly advertised. If you are working part time for a company, you may have the inside track to a newly posted position.

Internships

I know you may have already done several internships as a student, but if you are not receiving the job offers you desire, you might consider another internship after your graduate. Your exposure (with diploma in hand) to a potential employer might make you a job candidate of immediate interest.

Volunteer Your Time and Talent

Volunteering is always a good idea, and it might

even connect you via networking to a potential job opportunity. If you are volunteering, you will be helping those who will appreciate this evidence of your character and commitment. You will meet other volunteers, too, who may know of job openings. But more than anything, helping others is just a great habit to develop regardless of your place in life.

• • •

Finding a job is important, but don't stop enjoying your life. Take care of yourself in all aspects. Eat well, rest, and exercise. Expect this to be a process with some good days and bad days. Don't forget to pray often—you have a Partner looking out for your needs.

My *Do College Right* Checklist

o What will you miss most about being a college student?

o What are you looking forward to most when no longer a college student?

o Write down five positions you are qualified for.

Collegiate True or False

False. Use every possible opportunity to network to find a job—including all social media. Just be professional and appropriate while doing so.

014

Graduate School

AFTER ALL THE HARD WORK AND resources you've expended to obtain your bachelor's degree, the last thing you may want to hear is the question, "So, are you thinking about grad school?" I'll try to help you answer this question in this chapter.

Undergraduate degrees are about discovery; graduate degrees are about specializing in and developing a higher-level skill set. For most students, the undergraduate experience is not about becoming an expert, but rather about solidifying your identity, growing in self-discipline, and learning how to better analyze—all through a well-rounded exposure to various topics and experiences. In some fields, education for example, the bachelor's degree will definitely launch you into a teaching career, but in other disciplines, it may be almost necessary to obtain a graduate degree so that you can launch your career.

This chapter will help you decide which path to take—graduate school now, graduate school later, or graduate school never. My own path to a graduate degree fell in the "later" category. It also involved a career change—an event that may make obtaining an advanced degree a necessity. After a number of years in broadcasting, I felt a call to enter local church ministry. I realized that more education would be essential in order to become a lead pastor. I went looking for a graduate program that would provide me with a blend of church history, biblical studies, and leadership. It took some effort, but eventually I found exactly what I desired. I then enrolled and eventually earned my doctorate in ministry. I think the important principle that emerged from my experience is that you should really be clear on what you want from a graduate degree. Otherwise, it could be an endeavor that is disappointing and expensive.

Collegiate True or False

Even with a high undergraduate GPA, winning a graduate school slot can be difficult.
[Answered at the end of the chapter.]

"Should I Go to Grad School?"

Of course, there's no "one answer fits all" response to the question of whether or not to go to grad school, but let me give you a list of questions that might help you decide whether and when graduate school is right for you.

- Does your desired career path require a post-graduate degree? Will grad school provide you with a new skill set that can only be acquired in an academic setting?
- Do you really want to go to grad school, or is another person (parent, friend, professor) pressuring you?
- Are you willing to endure living longer with a low income that limits your lifestyle or the lifestyle of your family?
- How much more student loan debt will you accumulate in graduate school? Have you

carefully calculated the ROI of another degree? You may end up with an advanced degree and more student loan debt without improving your income-earning potential.

- Will a graduate degree improve your income? By how much? Be sure to consider both the short-term and long-term outcomes while answering this question.
- Will another degree improve your chances of finding a good job?
- Will you be able to reduce the cost of an advanced degree through a graduate assistantship or other resources that may not be available in the future? If you are already employed, will your employer pay for a portion or all of a graduate degree?
- Are you seeking another degree because you don't want to exchange the nice college life and schedule for the real, adult world?
- Are you certain that this career field (related to an advanced degree) is where you want to be for the long haul? If you aren't sure, it might be better to try to work in the field a few years and then decide if graduate school is a good choice.
- If you are married, does your spouse support you going to grad school? He or she may need to support you during this season.

If you have answered the questions above thought-
fully, I believe you will have a much clearer sense
of how to proceed. If you are certain you want to
go to grad school, but you aren't sure whether you
should go right away or go back to school later,
read over these pros and cons as you weigh your
decision.

Pros and cons of *going directly to graduate school*
after finishing college:

Pros

- You are in the "studying mode"—accus-
  tomed to the demands and unique life of
  being a student.
- You are very sure of your chosen career
  field and know that the master's (perhaps
  even doctorate) will absolutely increase
  your level of success.
- You have received guarantees of a graduate assistant position or other financial benefit if you continue (probably at the college
  where you were an undergraduate).
- The ROI for your future is positive with an
  advanced degree.
- You are supported in this by your spouse or
  other family members.

Cons

- You are not quite sure this is the right thing to do. You think you need some experience in your career field to make sure this is what you want to do indefinitely.
- You are tired of school.
- You are not certain the graduate degree will increase your income or opportunities in your chosen field.
- You will have to amass a significant amount of additional student loan debt.
- Your spouse is opposed and will resent the lifestyle sacrifices of your decision.

• • •

If you have decided to go to graduate school, keep in mind that you need to re-launch most of the process I described earlier in this book in regard to your undergraduate experience. The competition for graduate school is intense, so get started early in your search.

My *Do College Right* Checklist

- o Put pencil to paper to evaluate how much graduate school will cost financially—not just in additional college expense but in lost income—compared to future earnings.
- o Make a pros and cons list about grad school that is specific to your situation.

Collegiate True or False

True. Competition is intense for graduate school slots, especially at elite schools and in certain disciplines. This is another reason to start the application early and to carefully choose schools where your chances are enhanced.

015

A Lifelong Journey

PLEASE REMEMBER THIS IF NOTHING else: *education is not a place you go; education is your life.* In this book I have shared what I consider the nuts and bolts of how you can have an enjoyable college experience or, if your diploma is already in your hand, launch into a career that will be both personally gratifying and provide you with a good standard of living. In conclusion, I want to return to the theme I raised at the very beginning of this book: the importance of knowing, developing, and living in your divine design.

Each one of us has a divine design, a unique set of gifts, talents, and experiences that sets us apart from one another. I believe so strongly that everyone has been built to face and solve a unique problem in this world.

If you are just entering college, I sincerely hope that your time in school will speed you down the path to a deeper understanding of how you are wired, what your passions are, and how you will participate in serving others and making a contribution to society. College is just the beginning. The full realization of your divine design is a lifelong project, an endeavor that requires you to stay alert and be a lifelong learner.

This point of transition and change for you is probably as uncomfortable as it is exciting. No one really enjoys being nudged or pulled out of a comfort zone, but it's in these times of stretching that our divine Designer can accomplish great breakthroughs in us. I urge you to overcome any fears as you step into the next season of your journey.

I am confident that your best days are ahead of you. I believe that, wherever you are in your journey, you are a divinely-designed masterpiece who is destined for great things. That doesn't necessarily mean you will become famous or rich or powerful (although, in fact, it could happen); the true greatness I see for you, and every person, is the opportunity to live a life of significance and meaning.

The Adventure of Lifelong Learning

My belief, based on a lot of personal experience, is that the best way to lean forward into your future is to live a life defined by *adventure,* which is precisely how I describe where you are right now—whether you are just entering college or already have that diploma in your hands.

Open your eyes to a world that is filled with wonder! You are not limited by the expectations your present circumstances or other people have placed upon you. You are free to find something new and amazing every day you live. But you must be willing to see and experience life in fresh ways. You must be confident of what you know and humble about what you have yet to learn. You must embrace and cultivate the restlessness within your soul that points to the new—the unknown.

I cannot predict what your adventure will look like—neither can you! All you can do is embrace what is next. You can succumb to a crippling fear about the uncertainty of the future, or you can say a prayer and take the next step. I urge you to see your next season as a call to stay aware, to learn new things, to relish the adventure. It won't always be easy—life involves pain and suffering; you and I will not escape that reality. But it's in persevering through the difficult times that we uncover the richness hidden within the adventure of our lives.

So, will you embrace the adventure this season of life is giving you? Will you take on the challenge of always learning something new? I can't promise that everything will work out just as you had hoped—that's part of the cost of living your adventure—but I can promise that if you will stay alert and keep learning, you will come out a stronger person on the other side.

Collegiate True or False

There may be adjustments in your calling throughout your lifetime.
[Answered at the end of the chapter.]

The Qualities of an Adventurer

I promise this is my last list in this book! Here are some qualities you will need to cultivate in order to make the most of every adventure that awaits you.

Vision

Are you expectant about the future? We learn from the past, and we live in the present, but we place our hope in the future. This requires faith, which means seeing your life through the eyes of God's promises. In your life, you will face walls and giants that block your vision. The fears we experience in moments like these act like gravity, pulling our eyes down and away from the vision we've cultivated. Faith is what gets us through—faith in the truth that God is always with us and will never abandon us. I've learned that if I stay tuned into my design and the rich possibilities that may come my way, when something unexpected arrives, I can confidently say "yes" or "no" and not be tortured with any "what if" scenarios racing through my mind.

Self-Awareness

Moments of major transition, such as coming to or leaving college, are excellent times to examine how we are conducting our lives. Engaging an adventure requires that we creatively examine our attitudes and habits and ask ourselves: *Is this the best way to live my life? Is this habit the best use of my time and energy? Are there areas I need to grow in and things I want to learn?*

Right Attitude

Our response to adventure must always be "yes." Pride, arrogance, smugness, rigidity, victimization, self-pity—all of these are adventure killers. Humility and an eagerness to learn will prevent us from succumbing to bad attitudes.

Life Stewardship Tip #10

No transition comes without lingering doubts and the possibility of failure. And every phase of the decision-making process requires that we leave something behind.

Discipline

An adventure will always bring something new to learn and experience. This means adopting new ways of doing things. That's usually not easy as it requires exercising the discipline to learn and adapt. Such discipline does not happen by accident—it's a mindset.

Community

Adventure will take you to places and experiences that are new. The community you are a part of will either hold you back or push you forward. The Bible has it right: "Bad company corrupts good character" (1 Corinthians 15:33, NIV). Choose voices that will speak life into you and push you forward. Avoid the voices that encourage you to stay in the places that you are trying to move away from. Immerse yourself in a community with people that you want to be like. Your life will elevate to a whole new level.

Cultivate an attitude of expectancy. If you are open to the next adventure, it will find you. If you are not on the lookout, you may miss it and then perhaps have to deal with the "if only" questions. Be open to new things, new ideas. Be a reader. Look outside the box. Look outward.

Say "Yes" to the Adventure

So how can you be sure not to mess this up? Actually, you can't be sure. Part of the adrenalin boost that accompanies adventure is the possibility of failure. But here's the good news: some of the best learning experiences are disguised as failures. Remember, you are an image bearer in the tradition of that great saint named Paul who wrote that "we know that in all things God works for the good of those who love him, who have been called according to his purpose" (Romans 8:28, NIV). In other words, when we accept the call to the adventures that are placed before us, we don't have to worry about mistakes or messing up. We just need to be humble learners, seeking and following where God leads.

Living out your divine design isn't about always getting it "right," as much as it is about saying yes to as many adventures as possible. Trust me, most of the time there are more unanswered questions about what's "next" than there are answers. That is a big part of what constitutes the adventure. But what we do know is that we are following Someone who does have answers and has our back.

Over time, hopefully we gain a more complete understanding of our divine design and how that gives us our unique opportunity to contribute and make the world a better place—for others and ourselves. We just need to love the process, to say "yes" to the adventure. The choice is up to you. I invite you to accept the call to adventure—to embrace the exciting journey of being a lifelong learner. And I look forward to meeting you somewhere along the path.

My *Do College Right* Checklist

o What does being a lifelong learner mean to you?

o What fears—if any—do you have about the future? How does knowing that you were created for good works by a divine Designer alleviate any fears?

Collegiate True or False

True. I think life often surprises us with unplanned re-directions. We may go through periods—some of them quite long—where we just are not sure what the way forward should be. In those times, if we have the right attitude, our character is strengthened, our goals are clarified, and we lean more deeply into our faith.

A Note to
Parents

WHEN I LEFT FOR COLLEGE, I EXPECTED
my mom to shed some tears, but it was my dad
who really surprised me. He was not the type to
show a lot of emotion, but that day he had a hard
time holding it together. I think he realized that
this was a significant moment of separation—that
I was leaving, and we would never live under the
same roof again. All of the preparation he had
given me would now be tested. This is what every parent faces when the big day comes—all of
our parental input and guidance will now be tested—our children will be navigating challenges and
making their own choices. Now is the time to give
them freedom and space, to allow them to become

adults making their way in the real world.

But it still hurts! It's hard to give that last hug and watch your son or daughter walk away to begin a new stage of life. Many tears are shed on that long drive or flight home. I can't remove all the sadness—time will help heal that—but I can pass along some words of advice (much of it from Bethany Thomas, our vice president for Student Development at SEU[29]) that may relieve some anxiety, as well as help you keep the lines of communication open with your student. What follows is an incomprehensive overview on how to parent wisely during your student's first year of college.

Before They Leave

I do want to offer one brief thought on the months prior to launching your student into the college experience: Don't overlook some basic training in life skills—some things that your student may not have learned because you and your spouse have been handling these yourselves.

- Review how to do laundry
- Teach them how to keep track of a budget
- Go over how to back up their cell phone and laptop (using flash drives and the cloud)
- Offer suggestions for what foods need to be kept in the mini fridge

- Guide them on how to secure valuables

Here are some things that you can do to prepare before they leave:

- Be sure you retain copies of important documents—it may be a good idea to copy the student's driver's license, credit cards, and other important documents.
- Because of the high cost of college these days, a few insurance companies are offering tuition insurance. You may want to at least check it out.
- As far as what they should take with them to college, check out the lists online—there are many good ones. And, above all, don't let them bring *too much*! Your kid—and their new roommate—may want to purchase a few items of their own to make their dorm or apartment the ultimate home-away-from-home.
- Go to orientation. If at all possible, take your student to campus and stay for the parent portion of orientation. This is such a special moment for your student.

Move-In / Drop-off

If you are able to bring your student to campus, one of the first tasks will be the move-in—typically to on-campus, freshman housing. A few key points to remember:

- It will be chaotic; expect some surprises.
- Let your student lead the way and do the talking. They may do things a bit different-ly from you, but this is their time! You are there to help, not manage.
- Be ready to go buy something that was not on your list. You can run some errands as your student unpacks and gets acquainted with their roommate(s) or others on the floor.
- Show genuine emotion when it's finally time to leave—give the big bear hug and slop-py kiss—after all, you love your child, and this parting is a big deal. Some honest emo-tion is definitely in order (that goes for you too, dad!). Be ready to also share a few well thought-out and brief words of love and wis-dom—maybe even a letter to leave behind.

Safety

In today's world, all of us are concerned about the random violence directed against the innocent—often children. Believe me, as a college administrator, I know how important this issue is on my campus and at every college and university in the United States. Your student's chosen college should be all over this issue, but make sure your student remembers these basic safety tips:

- Don't do things alone
- Secure valuables
- Lock your door
- Lock your car

A part of keeping valuables safe is to be aware of identity theft. Instruct your student on the need to keep important personal information, such as the Social Security number, protected. If you have a personal identity protection service, consider adding your student to the account—typically the cost is minimal.

Health and Emergencies

During orientation, you and your student will be briefed on what to do and where to go if they become ill or there is an emergency—both at school and in their dorm. FERPA (the Family Educational Rights and Privacy Act) law[30] governs the flow of information about all students attending a college. If a student has signed their FERPA release it required that the university contact you in the event of an emergency. However, non-emergency information may not be accessible to you if your student has not signed a release. Most universities have an opportunity for a student to sign their FERPA release during orientation, however it is completely up to the student on whether or not they sign the release. In the case of emergencies, policies will vary among schools, so check out how your student's college will communicate with you if there is an emergency. At SEU, we provide transportation to local hospitals when necessary. Our university, along with many others, has a policy that a staff member will stay with a student until a loved one can come to the hospital.

Communication

At SEU, many concerned parents contact us and say, "My student hasn't called home in a long time. I'm worried. What should I do?" Prevention is the best solution to this dilemma: I suggest that you proactively set up a communication plan with your student before you drop them off at their campus. It could be as simple as having them agree to call you every Sunday afternoon or at some mutually opportune time. Most students prefer a regularly scheduled time rather than random "interruptions" from a parent. Having a scheduled time will also guarantee consistency in communication.

Not hearing from your student as often as you would like does not necessarily mean that something is wrong. This is often an area where you need to let some time pass and give your student some space.

Here are some other communication tips:

- Follow your student's college on Facebook, Twitter, and/or Instagram. This is a way to keep up to date on events and news without constantly asking your child.
- Be sure you know your student's preferred instant communication method. Be comfortable with short text or similar messages that may be random. You probably will not be talking on the phone as much as you would like. As you know already, today's young adults don't use their phones too much for calls!
- Don't neglect sending an occasional card, letter, or even care package. Those letters will be read and those cookies will be eaten!
- Communicate regularly but don't overdo it.
- Almost all colleges have a Parents' Weekend. *Go!* This is the perfect opportunity to visit in person and catch up. And they will like it that you came, even if this is not over-communicated to you.

Homesick

What will you do if your student calls and says through tears, "I just miss you guys so much—I want to come home!" This might happen, and since you also may be "homesick" for your child, you may be tempted to make this wish a reality. I urge you to resist the temptation!

In fact, I suggest that you never use the word "homesick" with your student. Your son or daughter may be uncomfortable or struggling with the adjustment to big changes in their life but not necessarily "homesick." Be encouraging, and for sure do not call and cry on the phone to your student about how much you are missing them. After a few weeks or so, maybe they can come home for a visit or you can see them on campus. Do your best to get them through these feelings in the early weeks and months. Grit your teeth and stick it out through one whole semester before seriously considering the decision to bring a student home permanently.

Friends and Roommates

You may pick up that your student is having difficulty making new friends or finding others to hang out with. Again, this is a fairly common issue early on during freshman year. I suggest that you encourage your student to try really hard to form new relationships and not lapse into long-distance communication with the "old high school gang." Those prior friendships can be maintained during breaks and holidays, but college is perhaps the optimum time to form relationships that often last a lifetime. A good way for your student to start making connections is to join clubs and organizations, attend dormitory mixers, and go to as many campus events as possible—without letting study time slide (see chapter 11 for more ideas on this topic). Most colleges assign resources to help all students get involved with others on campus.

You also may hear some woe about "the roommate." Roommates sometimes click from the get-go, but the opposite happens too. Sometimes it takes some time and effort to get the relationship rolling, so encourage them to be patient. If all else fails, roommate changes can eventually be made.

Studying and Grades

Sometimes we receive a message like this: "My student seems to be up really late almost every night of the week—are they getting their homework done? Are they falling behind in their classes?" Finding the answers to these questions will require some investigation. It certainly is not unusual for some students—even those who did very well in high school—to struggle making the adjustment to larger classes, less personal involvement from teachers, no prompting from parents, and more difficult subject matter. However, all institutions of higher education are concerned with helping students make a successful transition academically from high school to college.

At SEU, we have a tutoring center that will help a student set up a full-time plan for academic success—I'm certain other institutions provide similar opportunities. You can encourage your child to use these resources. You can also encourage your student to do as much studying as possible before, between, and after classes *in the daytime*. Students who put off all of their study until after dinner are often the ones who are up too late trying to concentrate when they are already tired from the day. Then lack of sleep contributes to even deeper fatigue and a vicious cycle sets in. Remind your child that it's better to study before dark—then hang out with friends and do something fun.

Finances

Being away from home and on their own often provides a student the first good opportunity to figure out how to live on a budget. Many students are not ready to do this and become easy targets for credit card companies eager to hand out their plastic.

In fairness to students, though, they often arrive on campus thinking they have accounted for all expenses to quickly find out that college is more expensive than anticipated. For example, required textbooks for just one course might almost wipe out their anticipated book budget for the semester. It's probably wise to have some type of joint credit or debit card account with your student early in the college years. This way expenditures can be monitored and adjustments made as needed. As with other topics, having the communication lines open with your student is also important with finances.

Faith

Elsewhere in this book I have discussed the importance of spiritual growth during the college years. Statistics reveal that many students walk away from a connection to their faith heritage during this time.[31] Since I am a Christian and know the importance of a vibrant church community, I would encourage you and your student to check out a church or two near the campus that might be a good fit and provide the support and encouragement your student may need.

You are in the stage of letting your student make the transition from dependent youth to independent adulthood. This is the time to let them fly and further build their character and strength for the inevitable life challenges that await them.

Your huge asset now is prayer! Occasionally, you may be able to offer your student some wisdom that they will receive. Now and then, if you do it gently and with grace, they may receive or even seek your advice. Share freely what life has taught you—but then let them go to find their own way.

Sometimes, though, even the best of us become overwhelmed by some life challenge. If your student seems overwhelmed, you may need to step in and seek appropriate help for your student until he or she is better able to cope with what they are facing. Don't hold back from contacting your student's residence advisor or others on campus if you are concerned.

Patience

No one grows up all at once—certainly not during the first year of college. Your student will mature, but in the meantime, there will be bumps and bruises. Your role now is to be available to pick them up if they ask for your help or it's a bona fide emergency. Learn the beautiful art of staying in touch without being overbearing.

• • •

Seeing your child leave for college is a stressful moment in life. There will be tears. You will grieve. But as a caring parent, this is what you have been working toward since you first held that child in your arms. Enjoy the moment of watching someone you love make the exhilarating leap into responsible adulthood. Now you have more time to focus on your marriage, on other family members, on yourself. Make the most of it!

Appendix

Campus Visit Culture Checklist

○ **Visit the admissions office.** This should be scheduled for you—you need to find out the status of your application (if you've applied). How is financial aid looking? Ask any questions you may have about anything!

Impressions:

○ **Talk to as many students as possible. Be bold!** Don't just speak to students who are guiding your tour. Are people friendly? What's the stress level? Find out things like, how much do you have to study? Is it hard to make friends? Is there a lot to do on campus? What kinds of things do you do on weekends? Are there fun things to do off campus? Good places to eat nearby?

Impressions:

○ **Hang out where students hang out.** The Quad? Student union? Coffee shop? Bookstore?

Impressions:

◯ **Visit the office of your major.** This should be scheduled for you but if not, be sure to do this. Was it encouraging? Informative? Did you feel welcome?

Impressions:

◯ **Attend a class—ideally in your anticipated major.** Was it overwhelming? Informative? What was the professor like? Can you see yourself taking that class?

Impressions:

○ **Eat in a cafeteria.** Was there a wide variety of food choices? Did the students seem happy to be eating there?

Impressions:

○ **Visit dormitory and/or other housing.** Can you see yourself living in this place? Does it seem crowded?

Impressions:

◯ **Check your campus athletic, health, and counseling facilities.** You will want to stay in shape at college. And you may get sick or need some personal counseling. Does this school have good resources?

Impressions:

◯ **Examine bulletin boards.** Does it seem like there are numerous activities on campus of interest to you?

Impressions:

○ **What's the city or town like?** Do students seem to enjoy being off campus? Why?

Impressions:

○ **Safety.** Do you generally feel safe and secure here or do you have concerns? How do you feel in your gut about safety here?

Impressions:

○ **Are there good churches near campus?** You may have to find this out from students.

Impressions:

○ **People vibes.** Now that you've spent some time in the student population, are these students the kind of people you could hang with?

Impressions:

○ **Other?** Write down anything and everything that comes to mind. What did you really like here? What was not so pleasant? Where does this college rank among your top three?

Impressions:

Endnotes

1. Shapiro, D., Dundar, A., Huie, F., Wakhungu, P.K., Yuan, X., Nathan, A. & Bhimdiwali, A. (2017, December). Completing College: A National View of Student Completion Rates – Fall 2011 Cohort (Signature Report No. 14). Herndon, VA: National Student Clearinghouse Research Center. https://nscresearchcenter.org/wp-content/uploads/SignatureReport14_Final.pdf.

2. HIGHER EDUCATION: "Students Need More Information to Help Reduce Challenges in Transferring College Credits," GAO-17-574: Published: Aug 14, 2017. Publicly Released: Sep 13, 2017. https://www.gao.gov/products/GAO-17-574?utm_medium=email&utm_source=govdelivery.

3. *This Adventure Called Life: Discovering Your Divine Design.* Springfield, MO: Influence Resources, 2013.

4. "School Shootings in 2018: How Many and Where," Education Week, February 5, 2019 | Updated: April 9, 2019. https://www.edweek.org/ew/section/multimedia/school-shootings-2018-how-many-where.html.

5. "The Tools You Need for Campus Safety and Security Analysis," Campus Safety and Security, US Department of Education. https://ope.ed.gov/campussafety/#/.

6. "Average Student Loan Debt in the U.S., 2019 Statistics," Nitro. https://www.nitrocollege.com/research/average-%20student-loan-debt#student-vs-credit-auto .

7. Judith Scott-Clayton, "The looming student loan default crisis is worse than we thought," Evidence Speaks Reports, Economic Studies at Brookings. Vol 2, #34 January 10, 2018. https://www.brookings.edu/wp-content/uploads/2018/01/scott-clayton-report.pdf.

8. Sauter, Michael B. "Here's the Average Cost of College Tuition Every Year since 1971." USA Today. May 18, 2019.

Accessed June 25, 2019. https://www.usatoday.com/story/money/2019/05/18/cost-of-college-the-year-you-were-born/39479153/

9. Amelia Josephson, "The Average Salary by Education Level," Smart Asset, May 15, 2018. https://smartasset.com/retirement/the-average-salary-by-education-level.

10. "Highest Paying Jobs With a Bachelor's Degree," College Salary Report. https://www.payscale.com/college-salary-report/majors-that-pay-you-back/bachelors/page/23.

11. "Highest Paying Bachelor's Degrees | Payscale". 2018. Payscale.Com. https://www.payscale.com/college-salary-report/majors-that-pay-you-back/bachelors/page/23.

12. David Shephardson, "CEOs tell Trump they are hiring more Americans without college degrees," Reuters, March 6, 2019. https://www.reuters.com/article/us-usa-trump-workforce/ceos-tell-trump-they-are-hiring-more-americans-without-college-degrees-idUSKCN1QN2XO.

13. Richard Feloni, "IBM CEO Ginni Rometty said companies have to change the way they hire, or the skills gap will become a crisis," Business Insider, January 22, 2019. https://www.businessinsider.com/ibm-ceo-ginni-rometty-talks-new-collar-jobs-at-davos-2019-1.
14. National Center for Education Statistics, Fast Facts. Found at: https://nces.ed.gov/fastfacts/display.asp?id=84.

15. "Scholarships & Grants for College Students," Debt.org. https://www.debt.org/students/scholarships-and-grants/.

16. Anna Helhoski, "How Students Missed Out on $2.3 Billion in Free College Aid," October 9, 2017. https://www.nerdwallet.com/blog/loans/student-loans/missed-free-financial-aid/

17. Thanks to Margaret Miller. Quoted from: https://propel.seu.edu/transition-to-college-life.

18. "Beginning College Students Who Change Their Majors